The Shortgrass Prairie

THE SHORTGRASS PRAIRIE

Ruth Carol Cushman   Stephen R. Jones

Photography by Stephen R. Jones

PRUETT **P** PUBLISHING COMPANY
Boulder, Colorado

Pruett Publishing Company, 2928 Pearl Street, Boulder, Colorado 80301.

First Edition
1 2 3 4 5 6 7 8 9

**Front cover—Pawnee Buttes: Northeastern Colorado
Back cover—Spiderwort (*Tradescantia occidentalis*)**
Printed in Singapore

The following publishers and individuals have generously given permission to use quotations from copyrighted works: From *The Prairie World*, by David F. Costello, copyright 1969. Thomas W. Crowell pub. Reprinted by permission of the author. From *Giants in the Earth*, by Ole Rolvaag, copyright 1927. Reprinted by permission of Harper & Row Publishers, Inc. From *My Antonia*, by Willa Cather, copyright 1918, 1936, 1946 Willa Sibert Cather. Copyright 1954 by Edith Lewis. Copyright renewed 1977 by Walter Havighurst. Reprinted by permission of Houghton Mifflin Company. From *Shingling the Fog and Other Plains Lies*, by Roger Welsch, copyright 1972. Swallow Press. Reprinted by permission Ohio University Press. From *The City of Saints*, by Richard F. Burton, copyright 1963. Reprinted by permission of Alfred A. Knopf, Inc. From *Centennial*, by James A. Michener, copyright 1974. Reprinted by permission of Random House, Inc. From *Pioneer Women*, by Joanna Stratton, copyright 1981. Reprinted by permission of Simon & Schuster. From *Black Elk Speaks*, by John G. Neihardt, copyright John G. Neihardt 1932, 1959, 1961, etc., published by Simon & Schuster Pocket Books and The University of Nebraska Press.

Reprinted by permission of the trustee of the John G. Neihardt Trust. From *Land of the Spotted Eagle*, by Luther Standing Bear, copyright 1978. Reprinted by permission of Bison Books, University of Nebraska Press. From *Sod and Stubble*, by John Ise, copyright 1968. Reprinted by permission of Bison Books, University of Nebraska Press. From *Charles Goodnight: Cowman & Plainsman*, by J. Evetts Haley. Copyright © 1949 by the University of Oklahoma Press. From *Indian Oratory: Famous Speeches by Noted Indian Chieftains*, by W. C. Vanderwerth. Copyright © 1971 by the University of Oklahoma Press. From *Life of George Bent: Written From His Letters*, by George E. Hyde. Copyright © 1968 by the University of Oklahoma Press. From *Pioneer Surveyor-Frontier Lawyer: The Personal Narrative of O. W. Williams*, edited by S. D. Myres, copyright 1966 by Texas Western Press of the University of Texas at El Paso. From "A Woman on the Buffalo Range" by Ernest Lee, from the 1960 yearbook of the West Texas Historical Association Yearbook.

Library of Congress Cataloging-in-Publication Data

Cushman, Ruth Carol, 1937–
  The shortgrass prairie.

  Bibliography: p.
  Includes index.
  1. Prairie ecology. 2. Prairies. I. Jones,
Stephen R., 1947–   . II. Title.
QH541.5.P7C88 1988   574.5'2643   88-15112
ISBN: 0-87108-736-7 (pbk.)

Photos on pages 48, 67, and 92 by Ruth Carol Cushman.

Designed by Jody Chapel, Cover to Cover Design, Denver, Colorado.

To Nancy and Glenn

with love and gratitude

CONTENTS

ACKNOWLEDGMENTS

In writing this book we've learned many new things about the shortgrass prairie from many people. Knowing more about it has enhanced our appreciation of this ecosystem, and that is what we hope this book will do for you.

We have tried to present an overview of many differing attitudes toward and perceptions of the shortgrass prairie, and we hope our generalizations have not distorted the complex reality of it. In many cases we have simplified complicated theories and have covered in one paragraph something on which scholars have written entire books. The bibliography will lead to additional sources on the prairie.

Our gratitude goes to the following people who helped make this book possible, especially to Nancy Dawson and Glenn Cushman who encouraged and supported us through many long months and who improved the book with their suggestions and criticisms.

We also thank the many people who shared their knowledge and love of the prairie with us: Dave Alles, Ann Armstrong, Karolis Bagdonas, Joel Berger, Richard Brune, Ed Butterfield, David Chizsar, David Costello, Carol Cunningham, William Dawson, Beth Dillon, Mike Figgs, Sue Galatowitsch, Grant Godbolt, Larry Hoeme, Jeff Indeck, William Jennings, Earl Johnson, Hugh Kingery, Richard Klukas, Jim Knopf, David Kuntz, Dale and Tom Lasater, Mary Ann and Willard Louden, Sydney Macy, Ron Ryder, David Schimel, Bill Shuster, C. H. Wasser, Betsy Webb, and Cheryl Wilderman.

We'd also like to thank the people who wrote helpful letters or shared information with us through phone conversations: Durward Allen, Johnny Beall, Alton Bryant, Earl Hess, Leonard Jurgens, Kathleen Keeler, Bill Lauenroth, William Mott, David Ode, Brian Sindelar, James Stubbendieck, Lois Webster, John Weeks, and Warren Whitman. We appreciate the fact that many of the people above also read our text for accuracy. Others we'd like to thank for reading chapters are Brian Jones, Patricia Limerick, Ben Lo Bue, and Joe and Pam Piombino. Finally, we thank Sandra McNew, who brought the prairie to life; Kay and Bill Jones, whose love and understanding made this project possible; Carol Sheppard, who typed and corrected much of the manuscript, and the Grover Market Basket, which provided good food and shelter from Pawnee thunderstorms.

Shortgrass Prairie

 Midgrass Prairie

 Tallgrass Prairie

Approximate extent of Shortgrass, Midgrass, and Tallgrass Prairie in the United States prior to 1850.

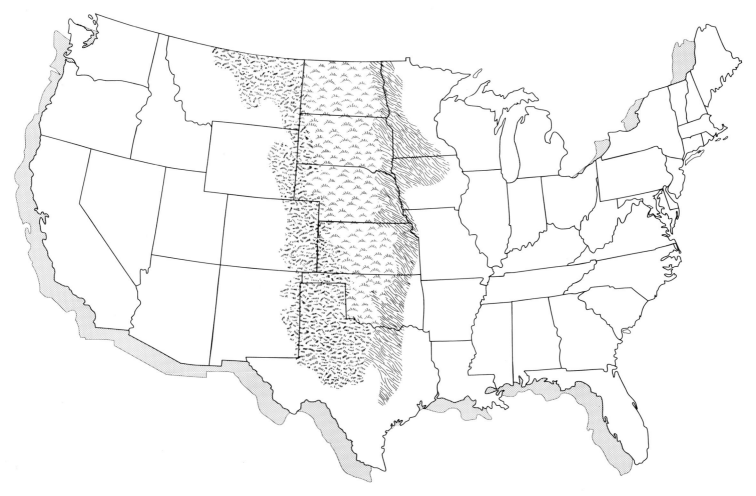

CHAPTER ONE

> There was nothing but land: not a country at all, but the material out of which countries are made.
> —Willa Cather, *My Antonia*

An Ocean Of Grass

Shortgrass, midgrass, tallgrass —these all form a part of the ocean of grass we call prairie. But what else does it take to make a prairie? And why are there prairies?

The Arikara, a Plains Indian tribe, made up a creation story to account for it. Below the sky world, they say, two ducks swam at peace in an endless lake. Suddenly Wolf-Man and Lucky-Man came upon this idyllic scene. They asked the ducks to dive into the lake and bring up some mud to make an earth. From this mud Wolf-Man fashioned the prairie for animals to live in, and Lucky-Man molded hills and valleys for people.

Emily Dickinson also mused about the prairie's origin: "To make a prairie it takes a clover and one bee— / And revery. / The revery alone will do / If bees are few."

A poem and a legend try to explain symbolically what makes a prairie. But of course it takes more than a clover, a bee, revery, mud, and Wolf-Man to make a prairie. It takes eons of time to form the land, soils,

Left—
Autumn evening: Pawnee National Grassland, Colorado

1

and plants. It takes water, wind, fire, and grazing animals to make up the vast grasslands of America. And it takes people—minus revery—to destroy the millions of acres of grassland that once covered the interior of our country like an inland sea.

Many people, when they think of the prairie, think of monotony, of an endless ocean of grass stretching from horizon to horizon. Perhaps in their mind they see something similar to the land called "Llano Estacado"—"the Staked Plains"—a place in Texas so lacking in landmarks that, according to the early trader and historian Josiah Gregg, Mexican traders and hunters drove stakes into the ground to mark their return trip.

Perhaps they picture herds of buffalo, a prairie dog town, and a meadowlark singing from a wire. If they remember the history of the West, they think of the Plains Indians and their conflict with encroaching European settlers, of covered wagons called prairie schooners following the Oregon Trail and leaving countless graves in their wake, of early explorers like Stephen Long and John Charles Frémont, of sod houses and the Dust Bowl.

The first explorers and writers to visit the plains, like today's travelers, varied in their reactions to the prairies. In *The Oregon Trail* Francis Parkman calls it "a barren, trackless waste, extending for hundreds of miles to the Arkansas on the one side, and the Missouri on the other." He describes this "naked landscape" in bleak terms: "Before and behind us, the level monotony of the plain was unbroken as far as the eye could reach. Sometimes it glared in the sun, an expanse of hot, bare sand; sometimes it was veiled by long coarse grass. Skulls and whitening bones of buffalo were scattered everywhere."

John Charles Frémont, on the other hand, wrote in his *Narratives of Exploration and Adventure*: "The grand simplicity of the prairie is its peculiar beauty, and its occurring events are peculiar and of their own kind. The uniformity is never sameness, and in his exhilaration the voyager feels even the occasional field of red grass waving in the breeze pleasant to his eye. And whatever the object may be—whether horseman, or antelope, or buffalo—that breaks the distant outline of the prairie, the surrounding circumstances . . . give it a special interest."

Almost everyone who wrote of the prairie compared it to the ocean. In *My Antonia* Willa Cather wrote: "The grass was the country, as the water is the sea. The red of the grass made all the great prairie the colour of wine-stains, or of certain seaweeds when they are first washed up. And there was so much motion in it; the whole country seemed, somehow, to be running."

Left—
Eroded sandstones: Toadstool
Park, Oglala National
Grassland, Nebraska

All of these impressions—beauty and barrenness, serenity and turmoil—are part of the prairie, but there is much more. The diversity of the prairie is more subtle and grows on the observer more slowly than the dramatic scenery of the mountains or a rugged coastline. In this book we hope to show some of the grandeur and some of the small, secret delights of one type of prairie that has been neglected in the literature on grasslands: the shortgrass prairie.

Prairies in the Great Plains generally fall into three main types: tallgrass (over four feet tall), midgrass or mixed prairie (between two and four feet), and shortgrass (less than two feet). The amount of soil moisture, the season of precipitation, and the relative humidity determine which type dominates in a given region, but the boundaries are not fixed absolutely. Like ocean waves, the prairie edges advance and retreat. In dry years, the taller species are less abundant and the hardier shortgrasses spread out. In wetter years, the tide reverses. And within each type of prairie, "islands" of the other types occur wherever differing micro-environments are found.

The map on page viii shows the approximate range of these three prairie types. Although most of the historic tallgrass prairie has been plowed and planted with assorted crops and cities, it once covered much of Iowa, Illinois, Minnesota, and the eastern edges

Left—
Windmill: Pawnee National
Grassland, Colorado

of Kansas, Nebraska, South Dakota, North Dakota, and parts of Canada.

Some scientists believe the midgrass prairie—which occupies parts of north-central Texas, Oklahoma, Nebraska, Kansas, and most of the Dakotas—is not a separate entity but merely a transition zone between the tallgrass and the shortgrass. Others say that parts of the shortgrass prairie are simply overgrazed midgrass. It's easy to get into an argument on the subject.

The shortgrass prairie is bounded sharply on the west by the Rocky Mountains, but on the east it merges in a somewhat desultory way into the midgrass. The largest expanses are found in eastern Colorado, eastern Wyoming, and eastern New Mexico. Smaller tracts occur in western Kansas, western Nebraska, the western edge of the Dakotas, and in parts of Montana, Texas, and the Oklahoma panhandle.

What exactly makes a shortgrass prairie different from the others? Low precipitation is the chief determining factor; the shortgrass prairie gets 10 to 21 inches a year, falling mainly from May through July. In cool Montana 10 inches may suffice, whereas in Colorado 14 inches may be needed, and in Texas, where evaporation is rapid, it may take 21 inches. The tallgrass requires 25 to 39 inches a year, and the midgrass 14 to 24 inches.

Wind and hail, also important climatic factors, flay

the sparse vegetation and frequently drive the inhabitants to despair. The wind, which has been measured at higher velocities on the shortgrass than on any of the other types of prairie, is mentioned in almost all the early accounts of travel on the prairie and is still endured by those of us who choose to camp or live there.

In his book *The Prairie World*, David Costello says that he and his research colleagues made up their own wind scales:

A strong breeze of twenty-five to thirty miles per hour tossed the horned larks in the air. . . . In autumn the Russian thistles ran freely before the wind at thirty miles per hour and pushed down fences by concerted action at seventy miles per hour. At forty to fifty miles

Below—
Winter sunset: Thunder Basin
National Grassland, Wyoming

per hour dust clouds streamed off fields like smoke from vast stationary fires. . . . At seventy to one hundred miles per hour, when the Chinook blew, tin roofs from cow sheds sailed into the sky, twisting and turning like kites with broken strings. The Chinook lifted ducks from their acre-sized rafts on frozen lakes and made them fly backward. . . .

During the Dust Bowl, Ann Marie Low exclaimed in her diary, "Talk about wind! Most of the scenery is in the air." Another Dust Bowl woman remembered that the worst thing of all was "the wind . . . sometimes you just wanted to find a place to hide from it."

Vegetation here must do more than withstand an unforgiving climate; it must also cope with poorer soils and less humus than exist farther east. Blue grama and buffalo grass, the dominant species on the shortgrass prairie, both spring from an extensive underground root system that is much larger in proportion to the above-ground plant than are the root systems of either the midgrasses or the tallgrasses. A square meter of shortgrass sod may contain five miles of roots. This root system enables blue grama and buffalo grass to adapt to grazing and drought better than the taller grasses.

Forbs, herbaceous plants that are not grasses, grow less abundantly on the shortgrass prairie than on the other prairies. However, that fact is hard to believe on a spring day when the fields are a crazy quilt of yellow, salmon, orange, vermillion, pink, purple, cerise, and blue. Evening primrose, yellow as a meadowlark's breast, may be partner to a magenta locoweed next to a sky-blue lupine, all of them bowing and swaying in the wind.

Trees can survive or even thrive in midgrass and tallgrass prairies unless they are suppressed by fires. In the shortgrass prairie they grow only in isolated riparian pockets unless they are cultivated. Lacking wood, the pioneers on the shortgrass prairie built their homes of sod, burned buffalo chips or cow dung for fuel, and in some cases even used stone for fence posts.

There are many examples of such ingenuity on the prairie. In her diary written in the days of hoop skirts, Mollie Dorsey Sanford recalled that when the precious hoops wore out, the women substituted small grapevines.

Use of sod instead of logs, stone instead of wood, grapevines instead of hoops are a few of the intriguing human adaptations to life in a harsh environment. The rest of this book will show how plants and animals, as well as people, have adapted—or failed to adapt—to what explorer Stephen Long mistakenly termed "the Great American Desert."

Early summer: Black Mesa
State Park, Oklahoma

Soul-melting scenery was about me.
. . . the prairie, whose enamelled
plains lay beneath me, softening into
sweetness in the distance like an
essence. . . . *this* prairie, where
Heaven sheds its purest light and
lends its richest tints.
—George Catlin
Letters and Notes on the
North American Indians

The Evolving Prairie

On the shortgrass prairie, the green hills roll away toward a distant horizon, uncluttered by buildings, signs, or paved roads. Pronghorn herds graze peacefully while prairie dogs chatter from their burrows. At night coyotes howl, horned owls call, and poorwills sing, just as they have for thousands of years. The land seems eternal.

Actually the shortgrass prairie is quite young, and it is changing before our eyes. The clues are scattered about: seashells exposed by wind and stream erosion in the arid hills of northeastern Colorado, isolated stands of ponderosa pine and juniper growing on bluffs in western Nebraska and eastern Wyoming, and skeletons of mammoths, saber-toothed cats, and camels unearthed in prairie caves and canyons from Montana to New Mexico.

The prairie, so often compared to the ocean, owes its existence in part to the ancient seas that once

Left—
White River Badlands,
Badlands National Park,
South Dakota

9

covered much of North America. The last of these inland oceans, known as the Cretaceous Sea, invaded the region about 120 million years ago. Its remnants are visible in prairie canyons where erosion has laid bare the old ocean bed, known as the Pierre Shale. Ripple marks in the shale suggest current action on the sea floor, and fossils of large mollusks, swimming reptiles, and enormous fish reveal the exotic fauna that once occupied this now arid land.

The Cretaceous Sea was warm and shallow but not a place for a swim. Fifteen-foot-long carnivorous fish patrolled its bottoms. Nodosaurs, four-ton dinosaurs resembling overgrown armadillos, waded in its shallows. Inland, where rivers meandered over marshy plains, the huge Triceratops and Tyrannosaurus roamed.

This was the culmination of the age of dinosaurs. They had flourished in North America for more than 100 million years. Dinosaur fossils are concentrated on the western edge of the High Plains, where uplifting and subsequent erosion of the Rocky Mountains has exposed sediments deposited approximately 100 to 225 million years ago. Some of the world's most famous dinosaur digs lie in this region: Morrison, west of Denver, Como Bluffs in southeastern Wyoming, Hell Creek in central Montana. In North America, as in the rest of the world, the fossil record for dino-

saurs ends 65 million years ago. This was about the same time the inland ocean began its gradual retreat from the heart of the continent.

The disappearance of the Cretaceous Sea coincided with the uplifting of the modern Rocky Mountains, a process that has continued sporadically until the present. Geologists still do not completely understand the causes; they believe shifting of the continental plates may have placed enormous stresses on the center of the continent, causing it to bow and crumple. Extensive volcanic activity accompanied this mountain building episode. Along the Continental Divide the mountains thrust upward as much as 15,000 feet; to the east the uplift was less severe, and the High Plains began to take shape.

During this period of uplift, the old ocean bed was buried under layers of stream-borne sediments, volcanic ash, and wind-blown glacial dust carried eastward from the emerging mountains. Wind and water ate away at the newer sediments, sculpting spectacular buttes and escarpments. The Pawnee Buttes in northeastern Colorado, the "chalk bluffs" of southeastern Wyoming, and the Badlands of Nebraska and South Dakota were formed in this manner.

Today these features provide welcome relief from the often monotonous landscape of the High Plains. Whether you find them beautiful or forbidding may

depend on your point of view or the time of year you visit them. In his novel *Centennial*, James Michener offers a romantic vision of the Pawnee Buttes through his heroine, Elly Zendt:

> They stood like signal towers or the ramparts of a castle, and they created such a strong sense of home that all of us halted on the hill to appreciate the noble place to which God had brought us.

John Charles Frémont visited the same country in 1842 after having spent several weeks dragging his men and wagons across the parched prairie. His opinion of the chalk bluffs, based on practicality rather than romanticism, may have been typical of travelers of his day:

> I had never seen anything which impressed so strongly on my mind a feeling of desolation. . . . The wind was high and bleak; the barren, arid country seemed as if it had been swept by fires, and in every direction the same dull, ash-colored hue derived from the formation met the eye. On the summits were some stunted pines, many of them dead, all wearing the same ashen hue of desolation. . . . We left the place with pleasure.

Whether seen as beautiful or ugly, these High Plains escarpments and badlands provide a fascinating fossil record of life during the past 65 million years. The White River Badlands in Badlands National Park, South Dakota, have been called the world's largest animal graveyard. The soft Badlands sediments are riddled with fossils, and rapid erosion ensures that new fossils are exposed continuously. Remains of more than a hundred species of mammals have been found, including those of extinct horses and camels, saber-toothed cats, monkeys, and alligators.

At Agate Fossil Beds National Monument in western Nebraska, paleontologists have excavated an array of fossils from a soft sandstone bench overlooking the upper Niobrara River. This site has yielded more than 20,000 skulls of Diceratherium, a pig-sized rhinoceros that frequented the area 20 million years ago. Mixed in with the rhinoceros remains are bones of Stenomylus, a tiny camel that stood only two feet tall, Dinohyus, a giant pig, and Moropus, a large, oddly shaped herbivore with a horse-like head, a giraffe-like body, and bear-like legs.

No one knows for sure why so many fossils are concentrated in the strata of the White River Badlands and upper Niobrara River sandstones. The animals could have been trapped in muddy marshes and sinkholes, drowned in floods, or killed during ashfalls from the violent volcanic eruptions that periodically shook the central Rockies. At Long Island Fossil Quarry in Phillips County, Kansas, paleontologists have recovered remains of four hundred rhinoceroses that apparently suffocated during an ashfall eight million years ago.

By looking at plant and animal fossils deposited in the same strata, scientists can piece together pictures of prehistoric life on the High Plains. The Rhinocerous Hill Quarry in Wallace County, Kansas, contains six-million-year-old remains of horses, saber-toothed cats, ancient badgers and ferrets, prongbucks, giant camels, peccaries, llamas, and rhinoceroses. Plant fossils recovered from the site indicate these mammals inhabited a verdant savanna consisting of grassy meadows, cattail marshes, willow thickets, and scattered groves of cottonwoods, hackberry trees, and elms. The shortgrass prairie had not yet evolved, nor would it until very recent times.

You can find evidence of the emergence of the prairie along the High Plains escarpments, where the "stunted pines" described so disdainfully by Frémont cling to windswept cliffs and outcrops. These straggly conifers provide a link to the late Pleistocene, or Ice Age, a time when climatic changes led to the gradual birth of the shortgrass prairie.

Just 15,000 years ago, toward the end of the Ice Age,

the High Plains environment still differed markedly from that of today. Open forests of juniper, pine, and spruce covered much of the region. Fourteen-foot-tall mammoths sloshed through swamps and thickets. Camels and wild horses grazed in grassy meadows and forest clearings.

As the earth slowly warmed and the glaciers that had once extended as far south as northeastern Nebraska and northern Montana retreated, the flora and fauna of the High Plains underwent a revolution. Within a few thousand years, the mammoths, camels, and other mammalian and avian species disappeared. Forests, savannas, swamps, and tundra gave way to prairie. On the western edge of the prairie, where the Rocky Mountain rain shadow limited precipitation to ten to twenty inches per year, drought-tolerant blue grama and buffalo grass took hold. Only on the high escarpments did a few pines and junipers manage to survive.

A typical "scarp woodland," as botanists call these islands of withering conifers, consists of a few dozen scraggly pines and junipers perched atop an isolated bluff in the midst of hundreds of square miles of prairie. These woodlands are home for some of the same bird and mammal species that inhabit the Rocky Mountain coniferous forest far to the west: white-breasted nuthatches, magpies, and even porcupines.

It may have been the sight of porcupines lumbering across the prairie that first caused scientists to wonder about the origins of scarp woodlands. How had forest-dwelling mammals found their way to these isolated tree oases on the High Plains? Had they wandered over miles of treeless prairie, worked their way along the cottonwood-lined streams that flow down from the mountains, or had they and the trees been there all along?

During the 1960s and 1970s, scientists dug into the prairie soil to measure the amounts of tree pollen deposited during ancient times. The deeper they dug, the more conifer pollen and the less grass pollen they found. Many of the deeper soils were those normally associated with forests rather than grasslands. The cumulative research suggested that scarp woodlands might, indeed, be relict populations from a much more extensive Pleistocene forest.

Why the trees survive on the escarpments is a mystery. Escarpments may provide conifers a safe haven from prairie fires or may be the only place where the soil structure enables trees to out-compete prairie grasses. At the moment these are only guesses, and further research will be needed to confirm them.

The fate of the late Ice Age mammals that once inhabited the plains is just as puzzling. Here the fossil record provides the only link to the past.

Scarp woodland: Pawnee National Grassland, Colorado

Scientists have unearthed bones of mammoths and other late-Pleistocene mammals throughout the High Plains. One recently discovered site lies near Hot Springs, South Dakota. During the late 1970s and early 1980s, paleontologists unearthed remains of forty-one mammoths and those of an extinct Pleistocene camel, bear, and peccary from an ancient sinkhole. The animals apparently walked down to a pond to drink and became trapped in the soft sediments around its edges. The bones appear to have accumulated over several millenia. The youngest were about 21,000 years old.

Little Box Elder Cave in southeastern Wyoming was first excavated in 1946. The cave, which lies in the foothills of the Medicine Bow Mountains, is a seventy-five-foot-deep, forty-foot-wide hollow created by the weathering of a sandstone cliff. Animals have inhabited it for the past 24,000 years. An assortment of pictographs on the cave walls, including red-ochre drawings of human hands and charcoal sketches of spear-carrying hunters, suggests several thousand years of human occupation as well.

Extinct species unearthed from Little Box Elder Cave include *Panthera leo atrox*, a huge prairie lion that towered over the deer it hunted; *Equus conversidens*, one of the last of the North American horses; and *Camelops histernas*, a tall, graceful camel. Many modern species also are represented, including pronghorn, bison, marmots, and porcupines. Researchers have removed 15,000 bones, representing more than a hundred species of mammals and birds, from the cave floor.

Several sites in Colorado have yielded mammoth remains, but the most famous is the Dent site, located along the South Platte River near Greeley. In the spring of 1932, a Union Pacific Railroad foreman named Frank Garner spotted several large animal bones along the bank of the river. Later that year Father Conrad Bilgery of Regis College in Denver initiated excavation of the site. The bones were those of twelve mammoths buried in the silt along the river's shore about 11,000 years ago. Nestled among them was an arrowhead, later identified as a Clovis point. This find was the first evidence of human-mammoth association in North America, and it was at that time the earliest known date for human habitation on the High Plains.

Because of this discovery and many similar ones throughout North America, the image of Clovis hunters hurling long spears at raging mammoths is now a familiar element of human folklore and history. The abundance of human-mammoth associations in the fossil record supported a theory, first proposed during the nineteenth century, that humans caused the sudden extinction of mammoths and other late-Pleistocene mammals about 11,000 years ago.

There were potential problems with this theory. As scientists unearthed more bones from late-Pleistocene sites, they discovered that many smaller mammals and birds had disappeared with the large game animals. They found that some game species, such as pronghorn, had increased in number at the end of the last ice age. Finally, archaeologists discovered human artifacts in North America dating back 30,000 years or more, long before the time when the greatest number of extinctions occurred.

Scientists began to draw a picture of gradual climatic change leading to dramatic ecological change. Pollen and soil studies show that the late Pleistocene climate was not only cooler than today's climate but also more constant. Seasonal fluctuations in precipitation and temperature were less extreme and regional climatic differences less pronounced. Under this climatic regime, "coniferous parkland," a mixture of open-canopy forest, savanna-like grasslands, and marshes, covered much of central North America. By today's standards, the diversity of mammalian life in this one, heterogeneous ecosystem was impressive. Camels may have grazed alongside bison and elk, while lions and dire wolves hunted the same forest clearings.

The Pleistocene parkland was replaced by an array of more homogeneous ecosystems, including the closed-canopy deciduous forests of the east, the dense boreal forests of the north, and the treeless grasslands of the Great Plains. Pollen samples suggest these modern grasslands were different in plant structure from those that preceded them; many of the grass species that the mammoths, mastodons, and camels depended on became rare, and the grasses that replaced them may have been unpalatable or toxic. It is possible these late-Pleistocene mammals simply could not compete with the herbivores, such as the modern bison and pronghorn, that had evolved with the newer dominant grasses.

Some experts still believe human predation caused the extinction of many late-Pleistocene species. In the June 1987 issue of *Discover* magazine, Jared Diamond, a UCLA physiologist, argues that gradual environmental changes could not have caused the sudden extinctions that apparently occurred. If climate were the cause, Diamond says, "we'd have to credit these supposedly stupid beasts with unsuspected intelligence, since they chose to drop dead at precisely the right moment to dupe some twentieth-century scientists into blaming Clovis hunters."

The exact cause of mass extinction at the end of the Pleistocene epoch may never be known, but the fact that mammoths, sloths, and camels inhabited the High Plains just a few thousand years ago dramatizes the potential instability of ecosystems over time. If the shortgrass prairie has existed for no more than 10,000 years, how much longer will it remain? Current research provides clues about the future of the prairie as well as the past.

Bill Shuster, a University of Colorado ecologist, is studying the genealogy of scarp woodlands in the Pawnee Grassland. Shuster chemically analyzes the genetic composition of pollens to determine the ancestry of limber pines growing on the escarpments. He hopes to pinpoint the origins of these forests and determine how well they are reproducing. At first glance these woodlands appear quite healthy. Evidence that they are stable or expanding could support the assertion of some climatologists that the post-Pleistocene drying and warming trend has slowly reversed itself during the last several thousand years.

Jeff Indeck, a paleontologist at the University of Colorado, is using a microscope and a computer to look at climatic change. Indeck analyzed the sediments deposited on the floor of Little Box Elder Cave, reading climatic trends by looking at how weathering altered the size, shape, and texture of individual grains of sand deposited at various levels. His work may help paleontologists to determine the age of

bones discovered at this and other sites, since we do not have accurate dates for most excavated fossils. According to Indeck, there are very few radiocarbon dated late-Pleistocene or early Holocene (modern period) sites on the Great Plains.

Recent discoveries of additional bones and fossils, including remains of ground sloths and mammoths dated around 8,000 years before the present, suggest late-Pleistocene mammals did not disappear all at once. "We tend to see a gradual decline. We don't see the wholesale extinctions," Indeck says.

Environmental changes, as well, may have been less sudden and more complex than previously assumed. Philip V. Wells, one of the pioneers in pollen analysis of prairie soils, made a remarkable discovery in southeastern Wyoming. Beginning in the late 1960s, Wells dug up giant stumps of pines and junipers from the now treeless Laramie Plain. Many of these trees had died within the last several hundred years. One juniper was four feet in diameter.

Junipers of this size are not found on the High Plains today, and junipers of any size are almost extinct in the Laramie Basin. Apparently the climate of that region is drier now than it was a few hundred years ago. On the Laramie Plain, a process that began during the last glacial retreat may just now be reaching its climax. Prairie ecosystems are still evolv-

Right—
Blue grama grass in autumn

ing as waves of climatic change wash over the High Plains.

Standing on the undulating prairie, as the grasses sway in the wind and billowing thunderclouds race by, it is easy to accept the illusion of being far out at sea. The prairie creates a sense of motion that can be both captivating and unsettling.

Edwin James, the naturalist who traveled with Frémont, compared the rolling hills of the prairie to "the waves of an agitated sea. The shadows . . . coursing rapidly over the plains, seemed to put the whole in motion, and we appeared to ourselves as if riding on the unquiet billows of the ocean."

The shortgrass prairie is moving, but in a more subtle way. It expands and contracts with fluctuations in the High Plains climate, extending its range during times of drought and shrinking during times of abundance. Long-term changes are difficult to measure or predict. Some scientists think the plains climate has grown slightly cooler and wetter over the past several thousand years, allowing the tallgrasses and midgrasses to slowly invade from the east; others believe this long-term trend is not yet clear. But short-term fluctuations are apparent.

During the Dust Bowl years of the 1930s, the shortgrass prairie crept several hundred miles eastward into Kansas and Nebraska as the taller grasses died off. At the same time, blue grama and buffalo grass, the dominant species of the shortgrass prairie, almost disappeared from regions of Wyoming, Colorado, and New Mexico. Willard Louden, a southeastern Colorado rancher whose family survived the Dust Bowl, remembers seeing the ground completely denuded of grasses. From the Louden Ranch at Mesa de Maya to the foothills of the Sangre de Cristo Mountains forty miles away, "there was nothing but cactus and European thistle."

Writings of nineteenth-century explorers and naturalists reveal the existence of the High Plains drought cycle. Edwin James, whose visit apparently occurred during a dry period, described acres upon acres of land where nothing grew but prickly pear cactus, forming patches which "neither a horse nor any other animal will attempt to pass over." The shortgrass prairie described in James's journals is a land of cactus, sand, and dreariness. There is no mention of the "soul-melting scenery" and "velvet covered hills" of Catlin's prairie.

The drought cycle helps determine which prairie plants expand their ranges and which die, wither, or lie dormant. In one way or another, all plants growing on the shortgrass prairie are drought tolerant. On the western prairies, where the drying effects of sun and wind are extreme, plants that grow close to the ground have an advantage. The leaves of blue grama and buffalo grass usually extend only a few inches above the soil, and their seedheads grow less than eighteen inches tall. These grasses conceal most of their anatomy. The bulk of the plant material, extensive root systems designed to catch and hold water, is underground.

The late John E. Weaver, who taught botany at the University of Nebraska for forty years, may have been the first to actually excavate and measure these root systems. From the 1930s to the 1960s Weaver and his students dug countless trenches, as large as twelve feet long and seven feet deep, alongside growing prairie plants. The image of Weaver, attired in coat and tie and using a pickax to untangle the maze of roots connected to a single plant, is legendary among prairie botanists. His findings were astonishing. Roots of blue grama and buffalo grass extend up to six feet underground and then branch out, growing horizontally for several feet. Roots of these grasses may comprise 90 percent of the plant's total bulk.

Extensive root systems help prairie grasses survive long periods of dry, cold weather. Blue grama and buffalo grass compress all of their annual growth into the late spring and early summer months, lying dormant the rest of the year. Some ranchers say grama grass can grow to maturity and flower in two weeks. This may be an exaggeration, but these grasses do seem to spring to life overnight after a late May or early June thunderstorm.

Buffalo grass is a sod-forming grass. Blue grama, which can form sod under certain conditions, is usually classified as a bunch grass. Bunch grasses grow in distinct clumps, with as many as a hundred shoots growing upward and outward from a single parent plant. Sod-forming grasses produce horizontal stems called runners and rhizomes. The runners creep along the ground and the rhizomes worm their way through the soil, sending out roots and stems of their own. These methods of growth and reproduction are critical during dry years when the grasses produce no seeds. Even in good years, only a few seeds germinate.

The growth patterns of blue grama and buffalo grass give the shortgrass prairie a patchwork appearance. Islands of sod are frequently surrounded by barren ground and cactus. Overgrazing and drought can augment this tendency. First-time visitors expecting the shortgrass prairie to appear as verdant as a bluegrass lawn may be disappointed. But to aficionados, the prairie—rough, uneven, sometimes barren—is always beautiful in its intricacy and economy.

Yucca plants manage to survive in areas where even

Below—
Buffalo grass

blue grama would have trouble gaining a foothold. James noted that the giant taproot of the yucca, "bears more resemblance to the trunk of a tree than to the roots of ordinary plants." He marveled at instances where the sandy soil supporting the yucca had been eroded away, leaving several feet of the taproot exposed. Indians used this fibrous root for soap, and they ate the green fruits that appear after the plants flower in spring.

On the cement-like sandstones, or capstones, holding the High Plains buttes and escarpments together, there are places where even yucca cannot grow. This unlikely niche is filled by the most ingenious moisture-conservators of the shortgrass prairie, the mat and cushion plants. Like mosses, cushion plants gather and hold moisture in a tangle of soft, dense growth less than an inch high. Large, carrot-like taproots anchor them to seemingly impermeable sandstones. Mat plants creep over the sandstone, sending out roots as they go. Moss campion, a cushion plant, and sandwort, a mat plant, grow in the alpine tundra as well as on the prairie. These ecosystems are geographically dissimilar, but they share the moisture-draining attributes of intense sun, desiccating winds, and rocky soils.

The hardiness of mat and cushion plants contrasts with the delicacy of their flowers. Moss campion and

Below —
Prickly pear cactus
(Opuntia *species*)

sandwort produce dozens of fragile blossoms less than a half-inch across. When these plants bloom in early spring, High Plains escarpments take on the appearance of perfectly planned, carefully manicured rock gardens.

Cacti and succulents, such as sedums, may also grow in rocky, exposed areas. They hold large quantities of water in their leaves and stems, and some have a waxy coating on their leaf surfaces, which reduces water loss. Shrubs with curled leaves, such as mountain mahogany, reduce the rate of moisture loss by minimizing the leaf surface area exposed to the atmosphere. Other plants trap evaporated moisture in tiny, silk-like hairs on their leaves. On the whole, prairie plants are lighter in color than plants growing in moister climates—a possible indication that prairie plants have evolved to reflect sunlight.

Drought, wind, and sun are but a few of the hazards to which shortgrass prairie plants must adapt. The High Plains climate ranks among the most changeable and violent in the world. Hot autumn days portend raging blizzards. Dry winter winds sweep across the prairie at speeds of 100 miles per hour. Summer days produce heat, wind, hail, and the ever-present threat of tornados.

Francis Parkman, who said the New England climate was "mild and equable" compared to that of the

Left—
Thunderstorm: Pawnee
National Grassland, Colorado

prairie, described a "typical" summer day along the Platte in 1846:

> This very morning . . . was close and sultry, the sun rising with a faint oppressive heat; when suddenly darkness gathered in the west, and a furious blast of sleet and hail drove full in our faces, icy cold, and urged with such demoniac vehemence that it felt like a storm of needles.

Early settlers often used exaggeration to portray the severity and changeability of weather on the western plains. In *Shingling the Fog and Other Plains Lies*, Roger Welch tells the tale of a Nebraska farmer who wrote to his brother in Illinois advising him not to come west: "As I was driving to town yesterday, one of my oxen died from sunstroke. Before I could get him skinned, the wind turned to the northwest and froze the other one to death." Another farmer claimed to have seen the same tumbleweed blow by his house three times in one day "going in three different directions."

The shortgrass prairie's climatic extremes result from its positioning in the heart of the North American continent. A constant tug-of-war exists between hot, moist air welling up out of the Gulf of Mexico and cold Arctic fronts racing down from Canada. When these air masses collide, violent weather results: blizzards in the winter, thunderstorms and tornados in the summer. The greatest temperature increase over a short period of time occurred in Spearfish, South Dakota, in 1943, when the thermometer rose forty-nine degrees in two minutes. The largest hailstone ever recorded fell in Kansas and weighed 1.67 pounds, and hailstones the size of golfballs are not uncommon. In January when warm winds, known as Chinooks, blow down the eastern slope of the Rockies, the temperature may rise to seventy degrees or more; during June and July thunderstorms, daytime temperatures may fall into the mid-forties.

Violent weather poses obvious problems for annuals, plants that complete their life cycles during a single year. Without deep root systems anchoring them to the soil, many annuals are particularly vulnerable to wind, hail, and drought.

Seeds of some annual forbs, such as low lupine (*Lupinus pusillus*), can lie dormant in the soil for years, waiting for the right combination of moisture and temperature. In fact, the record for the oldest seeds ever to germinate belongs to an Arctic lupine. Ten-thousand-year-old seeds, found encased in ice, germinated within forty-eight days after planting. Annuals increase their survival chances by producing bumper seed crops. A single common sunflower (*Helianthus annuus*) can produce several hundred seeds. An acre of sunflowers could scatter tens of millions of seeds over the prairie.

Because different wildflowers thrive under different conditions, spring colors vary from year to year, even from week to week. Wet conditions may favor the growth of bright yellow evening primroses and paintbrushes. Under drier conditions snow-white sand lilies may predominate. During some springs the shortgrass prairie appears drab and lifeless. During others the wildflower display is spectacular.

Like the perennial grasses, prairie forbs keep a low profile. In the Rocky Mountain foothills, spiderwort (*Tradescantia occidentalis*) grows up to two feet tall; on the prairie it ventures only a few inches above the soil surface. Other forbs, such as the groundplum milkvetch (*Astragalus crassicarpus*), crawl across the ground as if deliberately avoiding the drying summer winds.

For thousands of years before white settlement, fires raged over the prairie, keeping plant communities in balance. Fire probably killed off shallow-rooted forbs, providing elbow room for the perennial grasses. Fires, which the Indians called "the red buffalo," may also have kept woody plants, including pines and junipers, from invading the prairie. Lightning caused some fires, and Indians set the prairie ablaze to herd animals and to eliminate old grass.

George Catlin observed fires throughout the prairie region and noted that so long as a fire stayed in the short grasses, it posed little threat to humans or other mammals. The shortgrass prairie fires he saw were more alluring than dangerous:

> Over the elevated prairie bluffs, where the grass is thin and short, the fire slowly creeps with a feeble flame, which one can easily step over. The wild animals often rest in their lairs until the flames almost burn their noses, then reluctantly rise, leap over it, and trot off among the cinders. At night these scenes become indescribably beautiful. The flames are seen for many miles, creeping over the sides and tops of the bluffs, sparkling chains of liquid fire hanging suspended in graceful festoons from the skies.

In *The Prairie World*, David Costello described a twentieth-century fire that blackened 100 square miles of eastern Colorado. Gophers, prairie dogs, and coyotes avoided the fire by hiding in their burrows, while pronghorn easily jumped the fire line, where flames were a few inches high. However, a herd of cattle, grazing in a swale where grasses were higher, was engulfed in "house high" flames and severely burned.

How frequent were fires and how vital were they to the health of the shortgrass prairie? Sue Galatowitsch, an ecologist who helps conduct controlled

Below—
Controlled burn:
Lamar, Colorado

burns on the prairie for the Colorado Natural Areas Program, believes fire was a less critical component of the shortgrass prairie ecosystem than it was of the tallgrass and midgrass prairie ecosystems to the east. In the taller prairies frequent and vigorous fires may have been necessary to ward off invasion by trees and shrubs. "Fires on the shortgrass prairie were probably sporadic," Galatowitsch says. "Grazing, especially by bison, probably had a much greater impact."

The prairie of presettlement times was extensively grazed by large herbivores, including bison, elk, deer, and bighorn sheep. The role these herbivores played in establishing and maintaining the shortgrass prairie is not entirely clear.

Some experts, including Walter D. Graul of the Colorado Division of Wildlife, believe grazing is essential to maintain prairies in a "natural" condition. Graul observed that heavily grazed areas of the shortgrass prairie often harbor large populations of swift foxes and mountain plovers. Both are indicator species of the shortgrass prairie—that is, they are supposed to be found where true shortgrass prairie is found. He noted that removal of cattle from a shortgrass study plot in western Kansas resulted in "the plot degenerating to a condition dominated by sunflowers."

Others, including Galatowitsch, assert that studies of this type reveal little about grazing impacts on the original prairie. Simply removing cattle from an already overgrazed plot may not recreate presettlement conditions. The plot may require fifty to a hundred years to recover from the effects of overgrazing and other disturbances.

Prairie dog colonies once covered hundreds of square miles of western North America; there may have been as many as five billion prairie dogs on the High Plains alone. By burrowing deep into the ground, prairie dogs helped to renew the soil. Their grazing changed the plant composition, reducing blue grama grass and favoring buffalo grass and a variety of forbs.

Recent studies show that areas grazed by prairie dogs often yield a greater diversity of plants and can even produce a greater volume of forage than areas without prairie dogs. On the other hand, ranchers and range managers, many of whom consider prairie dogs "pests," can point to fields where these colonial rodents have stripped away most of the native vegetation. Prairie dogs do not exist in anything approaching a "natural," or presettlement, state anywhere on the plains. They are frequently exterminated, and most of the shortgrass ranges they occupy are intensively grazed by cattle. Thus, we will probably never know precisely what their impact was on native shortgrass prairie.

To truly appreciate relationships among living things on the shortgrass prairie, you have to get down on your hands and knees. Then an intriguing world opens up: large black beetles burying dung balls in the soft topsoil, tiny forbs pushing brightly colored flowerheads up through the shade cast by prairie grasses, white puffballs and fairy-ring fungi, springtails, leafhoppers, and walking sticks. Within a square mile of mixed prairie in eastern Colorado, David Costello once identified 143 species of forbs, 22 species of grasses, 10 kinds of shrubs, and 4 kinds of trees. A square yard of shortgrass prairie may contain a dozen species of plants and several dozen species of insects. A gram of prairie soil contains several hundred thousand fungi and several million bacteria.

The life histories of two rather nondescript insects, the pronuba moth and the scarab dung beetle, illustrate the complexity of prairie life and the mutuality of species. The small, white pronuba moth lays its eggs at the base of yucca flowers. As it enters and leaves the flowers, it rubs against the stamens, and thus carries pollen from one yucca plant to another. When the larvae hatch, they feed on the yucca seeds. The pronuba moth is the only known pollinator of yucca; yucca flowers provide the only known home for pronuba moths.

Scarab dung beetles roll pieces of dung into nearly perfect balls, lay their eggs in them, and bury them underground. This is remarkable in and of itself; the first time you see a jet-black beetle escorting a marble-sized dung ball across the prairie, you are likely to sit up and take notice. But there appears to be more to the story. Scientists are testing the hypothesis that scarab dung beetles play a critical role in germination of blue grama grass seeds.

Grass seeds are ingested by herbivores, deposited in their dung, and then rolled into balls by the beetles. When buried, these small dung balls may create just the right environment to permit the seeds to germinate and sprout.

In a laboratory experiment, D. T. Wicklow of the Illinois State Agricultural Research Service and Rabinder Kumar and J. E. Lloyd of the University of Wyoming spread fresh cattle dung and blue grama seeds on potting soil contained in glass terraria. Beetles were introduced and quickly went to work rolling the cow dung into balls. Within a few weeks, grama grass seedlings began to emerge from areas where dung balls had been buried. No seedlings emerged from other areas in the enclosures.

One way to appreciate the delicate nature of the shortgrass prairie is to look at its response to plowing, overgrazing, and other disturbances. In a 1974 study of old fields abandoned during the Dust Bowl years, B. Ira Judd concluded that these fields required ten to forty years to reach a state where shortgrass predominated. Karen L. Reichardt, who published a similar study in 1982, reported that the succession to climax vegetation is likely to exceed fifty years, and "plowing appears to have caused an indefinite, or even irrevocable, impact on the vegetation." A Colorado rancher told us that when he flies over the prairie he can distinguish fields plowed during the thirties from unplowed land. The old fields are a slightly different color.

Succession in old fields follows a pattern first observed by David Costello in a 1943 study. During the first stage, annual weeds invade the abandoned field. After several years, perennial forbs and grasses begin to replace them. It may take five to fifteen years before the perennial grasses become evident and ten to forty years before perennial climax grasses begin to dominate.

It is hard to determine when shortgrass prairie has reached a climax stage because nobody knows what a climax prairie looks like. Nineteenth-century explorers and naturalists paid more attention to Indian culture, weather, and other romantic aspects of the prairie than to what was at their feet. Grazing and plowing subsequently disturbed all the native prairie.

We do know that the shortgrass prairie is never the same from one day to the next. Left undisturbed over a period of time, it will slowly work its way back toward a climax state. As John E. Weaver said, "Nature is always trying to put back on prairie land the kind of vegetation that was there in the first place."

Below—
Mushrooms growing on cottonwood

CHAPTER THREE

What is life? It is the flash of a firefly
in the night. It is the breath of a
buffalo in the wintertime. It is the little
shadow which runs across the
grass and loses itself in the sunset.
—Crowfoot, a Blackfoot warrior
and orator, last words 1890

Wildlife

On a hot afternoon in the summer of 1878, O. W. Williams led a surveying party out onto the Staked Plains of Lamm County, Texas. The country was dry and desolate. A long drought had withered the prairie grasses, and undulating heat waves obscured the horizon.

The party had traveled six to eight miles along a muddy, shallow stream, surveying as they went, when the flagman asked Williams if he had heard a peculiar sound. A dull roar echoed from far off to the north. When the party looked in that direction, they saw what appeared to be a low-lying cloud. It couldn't have been a cold front, in mid-July, and it didn't quite look like a thunderstorm.

As the cloud drew nearer, small dark objects became visible at its base. The cry went out, "Buffaloes! A stampede!" But there was no escaping the approaching herd, which now stretched across the plains from the eastern to the western horizon. There were no trees to climb, and the wagons were a half mile away.

The men stood in single file, firing their rifles at the onrushing bison. A few of the leaders fell, and the herd split. The bison thundered by on either side, some so close the men could see the glint in their eyes and almost touch them with outstretched rifles. The men continued firing, almost certain they would soon

Left—
Bison bull: Wind Cave
National Park, South Dakota

be trampled to death.

Within a few minutes the roar subsided, the dust began to clear, and the herd, numbering perhaps 50,000, disappeared behind the low hills to the south. Where they had come from or where they were going no one knew, but Williams commented that this was "almost surely the last great herd of the southern buffalo, after they had been cut off from migration to the north and after five years of the Sharp's rifle in the hands of professional hunters."

Seven years earlier a buffalo hunter named Don Dodge related a similar story. It was reported by Will E. Stoke in *Episodes of Early Days in Central and Western Kansas*. In 1871, along with his father and his older brother, Wall, Dodge had gone hunting south of the Great Bend of the Arkansas River. Early in the evening, they set up camp along Rattlesnake Creek.

It was quite dark. While speculating upon how much farther they would have to go before sighting game, they noticed a sort of trembling of the earth; then heard a rumbling as of distant thunder, which became momentarily more distinct, and they recognized the approach of a stampeding herd of buffalo.

Getting behind the wagons, the men began to fire into the middle of the approaching line of huge dark forms hurtling down upon them. . . . The thunder of myriads of trampling hoofs, the click and clatter of clashing horns, and the bellows of crazed and demoralized animals was, he says, a sound that will ever echo in his ears.

And this monstrous pandemonium kept up almost the night through; and they had to keep constantly on the firing line, thankful indeed for their good supply of blasting powder. Some of the nearer animals were hit and tumbled to earth and were overrun and trampled by others which followed. But the herd was divided and passed on either side. Mr. Dodge is of the belief that there must have been thousands and thousands of frenzied bison in that mad stampede.

Modern estimates place the total number of bison inhabiting the Great Plains before the arrival of white settlers at between fifteen and twenty million. There were stories of wagon trains requiring days to pass through a single herd or of bison blackening the plains as far as the eye could see.

There were also tales of settlers traveling all the way from Missouri to the Rockies without seeing a single one of the great herds. Bison, like so many inhabitants of the shortgrass prairie, were nomads. They wandered almost continuously, searching for watering holes, wallows, and rich pasturage. Buffalo hunters often said that bison "liked to have break-

Left—
Bison calf: Wind Cave
National Park, South Dakota

fast in Texas, dinner in Oklahoma, and supper in Kansas."

Descendants of a larger, forest-dwelling species, bison were well adapted to life on the plains. With the endurance to run long distances at speeds of up to thirty-two miles per hour and the strength to fight off predators as large as wolves and grizzly bears, they were relatively safe in their open, treeless environment. Their heads were positioned low to the ground, and their eyes were wide-spaced so they could scan the prairie for danger and keep contact with other members of the herd while grazing.

For thousands of years, the strong social instincts of bison helped them to ward off predators. These herd instincts became a liability when white settlers arrived on the High Plains. The Plains Indians had learned to kill large numbers of bison by stampeding herds over cliffs or by driving them into box canyons. White hunters found they could pick off the animals, one by one, while other bison stood by and watched or ran along with the herd. Millions were shot from passing trains, their carcasses left to rot on the prairie.

Hunters had no difficulty killing fifty or a hundred bison in one day. Mrs. Ella Bird, who hunted with her husband in the Texas Panhandle during the 1870s, describes a typical buffalo hunt:

It was wonderful to me to see them kill the buffalo. The method they used in shooting them was queer. . . . When all was ready they would shoot the one that seemed to be the leader. They never shot them behind the shoulder, in the heart or they would pitch, buck around and break the stand. Always shoot far back in the body behind the ribs. This made them sick. They would hump up, walk around and lie down, then wait a moment till another led out. Shoot it then, another leader, on and on till you had shot several, then they would begin milling around and around. You had a stand on them, then you could kill all you wanted.

Below –
Mother and calf: Wind Cave
National Park, South Dakota

One hunter, Thomas C. Nixon of Kansas, set an unofficial record when he killed 120 bison in forty minutes using these techniques. In 1882 alone, 200,000 bison hides were shipped east from the northern plains. By 1895, only an estimated 800 bison remained in all of North America.

Today there are about 70,000 bison scattered in parks, private preserves, and farms throughout the United States and Canada. The National Bison Range in Montana, Yellowstone National Park in Wyoming, and Wind Cave and Badlands national parks in South Dakota contain some of the largest herds.

For the past four summers Joel Berger of the University of Nevada, his wife, Carol Cunningham, and a half dozen field assistants have studied the Badlands herd. Their base camp is a hailstorm-battered house trailer near the north park boundary. Berger, who specializes in the social behavior of ungulates (hooved animals), is curious about the effects of isolation on bison behavior, reproduction, and genetics.

There are about 500 bison in the Badlands herd, but a small minority of the bulls, the strongest and fittest, do most of the breeding. During the early part of the summer the bulls engage in head-to-head sparring matches to establish dominance. Later, when the cows come into heat, dominant bulls have their pick of receptive females. Since the Badlands herd is relatively small and isolated, Berger believes limited competition for females may result in inbreeding, which probably did not occur in the larger, free-roaming herds of the nineteenth century.

Each day members of Berger's team hike across the treeless, sun-scorched Badlands looking for the park's main bison herd. They may find the bison rubbing up against the sides of the trailer or roaming as far as seven miles from the nearest road. It can be incredibly hot—110 degrees in the shade—and there is no shade in the Badlands.

Once they have found the herd, the researchers pull out a stack of black and white photographs, "mugshots," and begin the arduous task of identifying as many bison as possible. It's important to know which animals band together and when. Each bison has its own characteristic horn structure; after a few weeks of field training, assistants can tick off the animals' names with remarkable rapidity. "There's Ogalalla, that must be Chunky . . . oh, I see Patches, and there's number 238." All this through a telescope at a distance of 100 yards. They spend the rest of the seven-hour shift recording the herd's social interactions in minute detail.

A male bison weighs as much as a small automobile, and, when provoked, can trample a human to death in seconds. Joel and Carol have had several close calls. Once while walking through a narrow canyon, they surprised a bull standing in a thicket. The bull charged, and they were just able to scramble up the canyon slope as he thundered by.

Such moments of excitement are offset by the tranquility and beauty of the Badlands in early summer: the lush green prairie grasses, fields of wildflowers, towering white thunderclouds, and fiery sunsets. Each night great horned owls and coyotes sing the research team to sleep. During hot days the antics of pronghorn, prairie dogs, and burrowing owls break the tedium of continuous field work. "It's a marvelous place," Berger says. "There's probably no place else in North America where the shortgrass prairie and the bison exist in anything so close to a natural state."

The bison is only one of many prairie species that were extirpated, or nearly extirpated, during the nineteenth century. Bighorn sheep, grizzly bears, elk, and even mountain lions once roamed the shortgrass prairie. These animals were eliminated from the plains. Packs of wolves followed the bison herds and gathered near the immigrants' campfires. To many, the wolves' eerie nocturnal howling symbolized the wild and frightening nature of the prairie. In a practical sense, wolves were viewed as competitors for wild game and potential consumers of sheep and cattle.

Pronghorn: Wind Cave
National Park, South Dakota

By the early 1900s, the last wolves had been eradicated from the Great Plains. Today gray wolves are found only in Montana, Minnesota, northern Michigan, Canada, and Alaska.

Even the pronghorn, popularly known as the antelope, was threatened with extinction before efforts by hunters and wildlife agencies led to its resurgence in the middle part of this century. Pronghorn are the only surviving member of the family *Antilocapridae*, which is unique to North America. They are more closely related to the European chamois than to the African antelope. Like the bison, they are well suited to life in an open, arid environment.

Pronghorn are built for speed. Their leg bones are incredibly strong, and their large forefeet are equipped with cartilaginous pads that serve as shock absorbers. Enormous lung capacity and oversized hearts enable them to run miles without tiring. Over short distances, pronghorn have been clocked at sixty miles per hour.

Their ruggedness, coupled with their ability to go days without water, enables pronghorn to inhabit desert country inhospitable to most species. As many as fifty million may have ranged throughout the western United States and Canada prior to the arrival of white settlers.

The early explorers and immigrants were often out-witted by the pronghorn; Lewis and Clark despaired of hunting them, and Clark described their gate as "rather the rapid flight of birds than the motion of quadrupeds." But there is a quirk in the pronghorn's behavior that hunters eventually exploited. With the pronghorn's quickness comes a certain boldness. When predators approach a pronghorn fawn hiding in the short grass, the pronghorn mother walks straight toward them, catching their attention, and then races off. Pronghorn bucks sometimes exhibit similar behavior. Hunters found that if they lay in the grass and waved a scarf or handkerchief in the air, pronghorn would sometimes approach to within shooting distance.

In *The Wilderness Hunter*, Theodore Roosevelt described how the "insatiable curiosity" of one pronghorn led to its death. After being frustrated in several attempts on horseback to run down herds of pronghorn, Roosevelt came upon a group of bucks that had been distracted by the barking of some prairie dogs:

This commotion at once attracted the attention of the antelope. They rose forthwith, and immediately caught a glimpse of the black muzzle of the rifle which I was gently pushing through the grass tufts. The fatal curiosity which so often in this species offsets wariness and sharp sight, proved my friend; evidently the antelope could not quite make me out and wished to know what I was. They moved nervously to and fro, striking the earth with their fore hoofs, and now and then uttering a sudden bleat. At last the big buck stood still broadside to me, and I fired.

Today about 800,000 pronghorn inhabit the prairies and deserts of the High Plains and Great Basin. Some of the largest herds can be seen along Interstate 80 in Wyoming.

A barren, gently rolling landscape, dotted here and there with herds of bison and pronghorn—this is a popular image of the prairie. A closer look reveals a remarkable diversity of wildlife, ranging from shorebirds to shrikes, from pelicans to prairie dogs. Francis Parkman wrote about this abundance in *The Oregon Trail*. While riding alone through a buffalo herd in what is now northeastern Colorado, Parkman became distracted by some of the prairie's other inhabitants.

The antelope were very numerous; and as they are always bold when in the neighborhood of buffalo, they would approach to look at me, gaze intently with their great round eyes, then suddenly leap aside, and stretch lightly away over the prairie, as swiftly as a race-horse. Squalid, ruffian-like wolves sneaked through the hollows and sandy ravines. Several times I passed through villages of prairie-dogs, who sat, each at the mouth of his burrow, holding his paws before him in a supplicating attitude, and yelping away most vehemently, whisking his little tail with every squeaking cry he uttered. Prairie-dogs are not fastidious in their choice of companions; various long checkered snakes were sunning themselves in the midst of the village, and demure little gray owls, with a large white ring around each eye, were perched side by side with the rightful inhabitants. The prairie teemed with life.

Parkman described one prairie dog town that stretched ten miles across the plains. These colonies were a focal point for life. Coyotes, badgers, ferrets, golden eagles, and ferruginous hawks gathered to hunt the rodents; bison paused to wallow in the dust where the prairie dogs had denuded the ground of vegetation; rattlesnakes and burrowing owls nested in the burrows.

The name "prairie dog" comes from the French "petit chien" (little dog). It probably was given to this rodent because of its highly social nature and its habit of "barking" alarm calls in moments of danger. The prairie dog's social antics, which are reminiscent of the play behavior of small puppies, captured the imagination of early settlers. Charles Goodnight, a Kansas rancher who pioneered the Goodnight-Loving cattle trail during the 1880s, was intrigued by the behavior of prairie dogs and even adopted one as a pet. Goodnight carried the prairie dog along on one of his cattle drives. During the day it would ride in the chuckwagon or behind Goodnight's saddle, and at night he would turn it out to graze. Said Goodnight, "The boys had a hell of a time playing with it."

Goodnight may have been the first person to write about the prairie dog's method of defending its young from rattlesnakes. He also exposed the misconception that prairie dogs, rattlesnakes, and burrowing owls live in peaceful harmony. His observations are quoted in *Charles Goodnight: Cowman and Plainsman*, by J. Evetts Haley:

> There is an old myth that prairie dogs, rattlers, rabbits, and little owls live together in the same hole. Owls and rabbits do use the holes, separately, after the prairie dog has abandoned them. When the rattler enters, his intention is to swallow the dog, which he does, and my observation is that a dog will not enter his hole when there is a rattler in it, which he probably knows by scent. I have put dead rattlers in holes, and later found them thoroughly covered up by the dogs. They evidently attempt to cover the holes when there is a live snake in them, and it appears the rattler is aware of this, too. If you slowly pour dirt in on a rattler, he will make his appearance promptly.

A more sophisticated version of Goodnight's experiment was performed recently by Richard Coss and Donald Owings of the University of California, Davis. Coss and Owings worked with the California ground squirrel, a rodent whose behavior is similar to that of the prairie dog. In their laboratory they introduced rattlesnakes into a glassed-in squirrel colony and observed interactions between the two species. When the rattlesnakes entered the burrows, the squirrels kicked sand in their faces and eventually built burrow plugs to keep the snakes away from the rest of the colony.

For the last several years we have observed burrowing owls and prairie dogs near Boulder Reservoir in central Colorado. The owls occupy abandoned prairie dog burrows in late April and early May. After the young owls have fledged in July, the prairie dogs either reoccupy the burrows or fill them in. Interactions between the two species can be comical. Sometimes the prairie dogs playfully stalk the young owls, and the owls dive back into their burrows when the dogs close in. When a prairie dog occupies a favored owl perch on a burrow mound, adult owls

Black-tailed prairie dog:
Boulder County, Colorado

will attack, sometimes clipping the prairie dog's head with their talons.

In September the small owls leave for wintering areas in Mexico and the southern United States while the prairie dogs remain. Though prairie dogs do not hibernate, they sleep a lot in winter, especially during cold spells. On mild, sunny days they make their appearance above ground, engaging in customary activities: family groups sitting on mounds preening and sharing food, sentries flicking their tails while barking out warnings, and males aggressively patrolling territorial boundaries.

Over the years poisoning, agriculture, and urbanization have taken their toll on prairie dog populations; but the colonies that remain are still magnets for other wildlife. At Wind Cave and Badlands national parks in South Dakota, golden eagles, badgers, and coyotes prey on healthy prairie dog populations. Burrowing owls still nest in prairie dog colonies throughout the West, with concentrations at Wind Cave, Badlands, Pawnee National Grassland, and Comanche National Grassland.

Elimination of prairie dog colonies has led one species, the black-footed ferret, to near-extinction. This small, sleek member of the weasel family lives and hunts in prairie dog colonies. Its agility and sausage-like body enable it to dart into prairie dog burrows, where it kills its prey with a quick bite to the neck.

For many years no one knew whether black-footed ferrets still existed. Then, in 1981, wildlife biologists found black-footed ferrets inhabiting a large prairie dog town near Cody, Wyoming. By 1984 the ferret population at this site, known as the Meeteetse Colony, had reached 128. That fall disaster struck. A canine distemper epidemic ravaged the population, and by November only 3 to 5 ferrets remained.

In the fall of 1986, Wyoming and federal game officials decided to round up the remaining ferrets in the Meeteetse Colony. By doing so, they were putting the ferrets' future entirely in human hands, hoping a captive breeding program would restore the population to a viable size.

Spring of 1987 brought some hope. Two captive females gave birth to a total of 8 baby ferrets. As of September 1987, 25 ferrets were still alive, including 18 adults and 7 young. Wildlife officials say they will wait until the captive colony reaches a population of around 500 before they begin to reintroduce ferrets into the wild.

Some scientists believe the ferret's susceptibility to disease may be linked to "genetic depression" resulting from inbreeding. If this is the case, efforts to breed ferrets in captivity could fail. A search is under way

Right—
Ferruginous hawk:
Boulder County, Colorado

to find other wild colonies.

The reappearance of prairie dog colonies in parts of the High Plains provides hope for ferrets and other species dependent on prairie dogs for their livelihood. During the past twenty years several hundred prairie dog towns have appeared along the Front Range of Colorado, between Colorado Springs and Fort Collins. Boulder County, alone, has more than 150. Each winter these colonies attract scores of ferruginous hawks and an ever-growing number of bald eagles. The eagles are more suited to scavenging than hunting, so they perch quietly in the cottonwoods while the hawks do most of the work. When the hawks make a successful catch, the eagles steal away the prey. A ferruginous hawk may lose a prairie dog to a bald eagle which then has the prey snatched from its talons by a golden eagle. Survival on the prairie requires perseverence and ingenuity.

You might think the numerous prairie rattlesnakes would have posed a substantial hazard to early day travelers on the High Plains. Parkman noted these "slimy intruders" could be seen "basking at all times" atop prairie dog mounds. But historical accounts of snakes biting humans are hard to find, except in fiction.

In *My Antonia*, Willa Cather's heroine barely escapes the fangs of a large prairie rattler, and in James

Michener's *Centennial*, one of the characters dies instantly when a rattler bites her in the neck. Attacks of this nature are relatively uncommon for a number of reasons. Rattlesnakes, which are shy, retiring creatures, lie in wait for their prey rather than stalking it. When alarmed they would rather flee than bite, and their bites are rarely fatal.

David Chiszar, an ethologist at the University of Colorado in Boulder, has been studying rattlesnake behavior for fifteen years. On spring weekends Chiszar likes to ride his motorcycle up to northeastern Colorado to gather live specimens for the collection he keeps in the basement of the University psychology building. In late March rattlesnakes that have been hibernating communally begin to emerge from their burrows. Chiszar once counted more than a hundred snakes within a few meters of one of these dens.

Dave Duvall, a former student of Chiszar's who now teaches at the University of Wyoming, has implanted radio transmitters in the body cavities of rattlesnakes after they emerged from their dens. He discovered that some snakes travel as far as ten miles before settling into their hunting areas.

In his laboratory Chiszar studies how rattlesnakes hunt their prey. Contrary to popular myth, rattlesnakes generally do not stalk small mammals; mostly they lie in wait. Rattlesnakes, says Chiszar, are "ambushers." "From an evolutionary point of view, it's good they don't chase actively about, following mouse trails and burning lots of energy. There are mouse trails all over the prairie. A snake could follow them all the way to Kansas before he found a mouse."

Instead, rattlesnakes lie camouflaged in a place where mice are likely to pass by. "The first thing the snake has to do is pick an ambushing spot. And that's kind of interesting, because you can think of it as the snake making a prediction about the likelihood of prey turning up."

Rattlesnakes are pit vipers; they have heat sensitive pits on their faces to help them detect the presence of prey. They use these thermal cues and their eyesight to tell when a mouse is close enough for a strike.

After striking the mouse and injecting its venom, the rattlesnake withdraws. Rather than trying to finish the prey off on the spot and risking injury to its eyes or face, the snake waits for the poison to take effect. Usually a mouse wanders off for several yards, well out of range of the snake's thermal sensors or eyesight, before it dies. The rattler uses its chemical senses, sniffing the air and the ground with its tongue to find the dead mouse.

Chiszar has shown that this chemosensing behavior is activated by the strike. When the snake strikes its prey, the prey's odor "registers" on the vomeronasal organ on the roof of the snake's mouth. The snake immediately begins flicking its tongue and follows the odor to the particular mouse it has killed.

Chiszar points out that the rattlesnake's hunting strategy is well suited to life in an exposed environment. "If rattlesnakes are all curled up in a hiding place, a shady spot, they're not burning up energy, they're not fighting thermo-regulatory battles, they're not exposing themselves to hawks. By being in ambush they're not investing calories."

Recently Duvall discovered a "rattlesnake rookery" in central Wyoming. In September as many as a hundred snakes converge on an area the size of a football field to give birth to their young. Where do the young snakes go? Duvall and his students are working hard to find out. Meanwhile, they keep the "rookery" location a secret.

Fear of rattlesnakes has led to their being persecuted to the point of near extinction in parts of the High Plains, but they still are relatively abundant in protected areas such as Badlands National Park. The common species is the prairie rattlesnake, which is found throughout the shortgrass prairie. A related species, the massassauga, inhabits parts of Colorado, Kansas, Oklahoma, and Texas.

Chiszar's collection of several dozen prairie rattlesnakes contains a snake that has a perfectly smooth, rattle-less tail. Rattles are fine for warning away herbivores, such as bison and pronghorn, but to people rattles serve more as advertisements than threats. Perhaps a new breed of prairie rattlesnake is evolving in response to the human presence on the High Plains.

The use of prairie dog burrows by rattlesnakes, as well as by ferrets and burrowing owls, illustrates an important aspect of prairie life: the difficulty of finding shelter in a treeless and nearly shrubless environment. Golden eagles, ferruginous hawks, and prairie falcons solve this problem by nesting on cliffs and escarpments. These species are fairly plentiful in northern Colorado and eastern Wyoming, where chalky bluffs rise up from the rolling prairie. Smaller birds, including the rock wren, white-throated swift, and cliff swallow, also inhabit these escarpments.

"Tree islands," small groves of cottonwoods beside streams or marshes, provide nesting habitat for Swainson's hawks, great-horned owls, western and eastern kingbirds, loggerhead shrikes, orioles, and warblers. In late spring and early summer these areas provide spectacular birdwatching.

Many of the birds that inhabit the shortgrass prairie nest on the ground. Grasshopper sparrows, horned larks, and meadowlarks often build their nests at the base of cactus plants and small "shrub islands." Studies of horned larks show that their young are able to tolerate temperature extremes that would be fatal to nestlings of other species. This tolerance is essential, since prairie summers invariably bring searing heat and frigid hailstorms. Because perching sites for singing are scarce, lark buntings give their elaborate four-part territorial call while on the wing.

Many shorebirds, including the killdeer, mountain plover, avocet, and long-billed curlew, hardly build nests at all. They lay their eggs in shallow depressions which they sometimes line with a few stems and pebbles. These species rely mainly on bluff and camouflage to deter predators. If you approach a killdeer nest too closely, the adults will greet you with cries, squeals, broken-wing acts (a maneuver whereby the bird feigns injury to distract predators), and other forms of organized mayhem designed to lead you away. Curlews and avocets take a more direct approach. On a recent trip to the Badlands we were attacked continually by long-billed curlews. They came directly at us, four feet off the ground, at speeds approaching forty miles an hour. Four or five adults would take turns on these attack flights, their comi-

Western meadowlark:
Sawhill Ponds, Colorado

Burrowing owls:
Boulder County, Colorado

cally large beaks bleating out continual warning cries.

One of the delights of the shortgrass prairie is the presence of bird species that seem totally out of place. One evening in early summer, while camping in northeastern Colorado, we were astonished to see a large flock of white pelicans fly directly overhead. Although pelicans nest on an island in an eastern Colorado lake, they did not seem to belong. Later that evening, the sky was darkened by flocks of Canada geese and ducks. The next morning, we visited some small ponds tucked into depressions, or "potholes," in the rolling prairie and discovered yellow-headed blackbirds, spotted sandpipers, avocets, great blue herons, and northern harriers.

For many species, survival on the prairie is a tenuous proposition. One drought year, a severe hailstorm during the breeding season, and populations may be decimated. Destruction of breeding habitat by overgrazing, farming, and other human activities has left many prairie species vulnerable to sudden extinction.

One threatened species is the lesser prairie chicken, which inhabits shortgrass and mixed-grass prairies in southeastern Colorado, western Kansas, northwestern Oklahoma, and the Texas Panhandle. Lesser prairie chickens were so common during the nineteenth century that millions were shipped back east to be served as delicacies in the finest restaurants. Today,

as farming and ranching eat away at the prairie chicken's fragile habitat, less than 50,000 remain.

The lesser prairie chicken is best known for its "booming" ritual, an elaborate and bizarre courtship display performed during early spring. Males gather on leks, or "booming grounds," where they literally "strut their stuff" before admiring females. While prancing, leaping, and rushing to and fro, the males raise their neck feathers and puff out two rose-colored air sacs, emitting an eerie, turkey-like call. The term "booming" was first applied to the low, resonant voice of the greater prairie chicken, a closely related species found in tallgrass prairies. The lesser prairie chicken's call is higher pitched, more like the gurgling sound made by pebbles striking water.

Fortunately, many of the remaining leks are in the Comanche and Cimarron national grasslands, where Division of Wildlife and federal officials closely monitor prairie chicken populations and breeding habitat. The chickens in the federal grasslands seem to be thriving, and there is hope that viable populations can be maintained. However, a 1930s-type drought or further habitat loss could be disastrous.

A species that is hovering much closer to the brink of extinction is the Wiest sphinx moth. For the past ten years, Karolis Bagdonas, of the University of Wyoming, and his student field team have been combing the prairies for signs of the moth. First discovered in 1934 by Ray Wiest, a physician living in Estes Park, Colorado, the prairie sphinx moth was not seen again until 1979 and was thought to be extinct.

In that year Bagdonas and his team, known affectionately among lepidopterists as "Bagdonas's Flying Circus" (probably for their habit of racing across the prairie to elude voracious insect collectors), found a small colony of the moths in northeastern Colorado. Since then, Bagdonas has carefully studied the moth's habits while taking extraordinary measures to keep the colony's location secret. Insect collectors keep a constant eye on the "Flying Circus," and Bagdonas has employed a variety of tactics to keep collectors off the scent, including setting up camp in the wrong location and detouring as much as seventy-five miles.

Prairie sphinx moths breed exclusively on a small primrose, *Oenothera latifolia*, which grows in isolated pockets of sandy soil. The primroses themselves are endangered. They require a constant underground water source, and their drought tolerance has been strained by the buffeting of the hooves of cattle and horses. Bad weather in recent years also has taken its toll on the moths. In 1982 and 1983, snow and freezing temperatures during the flying season appeared to have killed all the moths in a single remaining colony.

Fortunately, the prairie sphinx moth, like so many other inhabitants of the shortgrass prairie, has evolved to deal with climatic adversity. In times of severe weather, pupae of the moth stay in the ground, waiting to emerge the following season. This was the case in 1983, and in June of 1984 Bagdonas and his team found 25 moths, the first they had seen in two years. By summer of 1986 this colony contained more than 50 moths and appeared to be expanding. Meanwhile, scientists had collected prairie sphinx moths from other locations on the Great Plains, suggesting that additional colonies might exist. Whether this species survives may depend on the amount of protection it receives from federal and state governments and on the amount of encroachment on its breeding grounds in the future by livestock and humans.

Bagdonas's work with the Wiest sphinx moth may help scientists understand the causes of extirpation of other species. Over the millenia thousands of species have appeared and disappeared on the shortgrass prairie, including the mammoth, the saber-toothed cat, and perhaps now, the black-footed ferret. Today extinctions of species throughout the earth are occurring at an ever-increasing rate. "Extinctions are occurring at about 24 species per day. Twenty-five to thirty percent of all animals, plants, and insects will be extinct by the year 2020," Bagdonas says. "There's

American wigeon:
Boulder, Colorado

Sandhill cranes:
Gibbon, Nebraska

a big push just to classify everything before it becomes extinct."

Until recently most extinctions and near extinctions probably resulted from evolution and natural changes in the environment. Today pollution, overgrazing, desertification, and urbanization threaten the future of many species. On the shortgrass prairie, small changes can have disastrous results. Whether such animals as the lesser prairie chicken, the prairie sphinx moth, the burrowing owl, and the swift fox go the way of the gray wolf will depend on our level of commitment to their preservation.

In 1890 a Sioux chief named Kicking Bear spoke to his people about the extinction of the buffalo. He said he had talked with the Great Spirit, who had promised that the white man would be eliminated from the prairie and the land restored to its original condition:

> I will cover the earth with new soil to a depth of five times the height of a man, and under this new soil will be buried all the whites, and all the holes and rotten places will be filled up. The new lands will be covered with sweet-grass and running water and trees, and herds of buffalo and ponies will stray over it, that my red children may eat and drink, hunt and rejoice.

Kicking Bear's prediction may never come true, but the shortgrass prairie does exhibit a certain power to restore itself. In the Badlands, where several inches of soil have accumulated since the arrival of white settlers, herds of pronghorn and bison share the open range with prairie dogs and burrowing owls. Along prairie rivers and streams, bald eagles are slowly returning to nest sites abandoned during the days of Frémont and Parkman. We may not be able to resurrect the past, but with luck we can preserve the abundance that still remains.

CHAPTER FOUR

And I saw that the sacred hoop of
my people was one of many hoops
that made one circle, wide as
daylight and as starlight, and in the
center grew one mighty flowering
tree to shelter all the children.
—Black Elk, *Black Elk Speaks*

Footsteps Past

It was the grass, indirectly, that lured the first humans to the New World from Siberia. Lush grasses enticed herds of mammoth, bison, and other game to cross what is now the Bering Strait via a land bridge. And, inevitably, people followed the animals. Debate still rages over just when those momentous migrations occurred—20,000 or 40,000 years ago, or sometime later or sometime in between those dates.

Slowly the hunter-gatherers spread south and east across the High Plains. By the time Europeans arrived on the scene, some thirty-one tribes (including the Arapaho, Arikara, Assiniboin, Blackfoot, Cheyenne, Comanche, Crow, Gros Ventre, Kiowa, Kiowa-Apache, Mandan, Pawnee, Sarsi, and Teton-Dakota) were established on the plains. In many ways, the short-grass prairie shaped their way of life.

In *The Great Plains*, historian Walter Prescott Webb claimed that a nomadic, mainly nonagricultural lifestyle was the most significant adaptation the Plains Indians made to the prairie. A few tribes along the rivers planted cornfields and settled in villages, but most of the Plains Indians roamed the land gathering fruit, vegetables, and seeds and hunting bison.

Left—
Prairie View Community Building: Pawnee National Grassland, Colorado

51

Even village dwellers such as the Mandan and Arikara went on the hunt in summer after the women had finished planting the corn, squash, beans, sunflowers, and tobacco.

The bison provided everything from food to fuel to shelter to such conveniences as flyswatters made from the tails. The Indians used the hide as canvas for paintings and the porous knee bone for a brush, and children tied jaw bones together with rawhide to make a sled.

As long as the Indians relied on the bow and arrow, hunting required careful stalking. A painting by George Catlin shows two men crawling on their bellies wearing wolfskin disguises as they approach an unwary herd. Collective hunts with the entire tribe participating were more common. Sometimes they would drive a herd into a box canyon or into a three-sided stone corral; sometimes they would encircle the herd with fire; and sometimes they would stampede them over a cliff.

The Indians showed great ingenuity in devising tools and weapons from materials close at hand. They flaked flint, chert, and obsidian into arrowheads, spearheads, and scrapers. They used thorns from the prickly pear for bird arrow points. They fashioned bones into awls, hoes, and shovels and used buffalo horns for cups and spoons. They brushed their long hair with a porcupine tail, or porcupine bristles tied to a stick, or the rough side of a buffalo tongue. Sometimes they lined pits with fresh animal skins into which they dropped heated stones to cook their stews.

The Plains Indians made little in the way of basketry or pottery; perhaps such items were too cumbersome or fragile for people constantly on the move. Before the coming of the horse, they used dogs, their only domestic animal, to transport their belongings. They attached two poles to the dogs' shoulders and

Below—
Bison herd: Wind Cave
National Park, South Dakota

lashed a bundle, which might weigh up to 150 pounds, onto a rough frame. Anything that would not fit onto this "travois" was carried by the women.

Their homes were also suitable to a treeless environment that could fluctuate between extremes of heat and cold. Some of the semisedentary tribes built circular, dome-shaped earthlodges that could house up to forty people plus horses. However, the cone-shaped tepee made from buffalo hide is the best known of all Indian dwellings. Designed with an inside skin to trap a layer of dead air for insulation and with a smoke vent in the center, the tepee provided a comfortable refuge from either storm or sun. The explorer Frémont wrote: "Such a lodge, when properly pitched, is, from its conical form, almost perfectly secure against the violent winds which are frequent in this region, and, with a fire in the center, is a dry and warm shelter in bad weather. By raising the lower part so as to permit the breeze to pass freely, it is converted into a pleasant summer residence, with the extraordinary advantage of being entirely free from mosquitoes." Ideal for a nomadic life, the tepee was easily dismantled, and its poles and hide formed the travois when it was time to move on.

Because of their nomadic way of life, the Plains Indians had to communicate with different tribes that spoke different languages. They also had to communicate with each other across great distances; and, if they were on a hunt or war party, silence was necessary. These circumstances led to the development of a sign and gesture language perfectly suited to the vast expanses of the High Plains. They also used smoke, blanket, and horse signals, and, until the whites introduced the mirror, they signaled with flakes of obsidian reflecting the sun.

The prairie also influenced the Indians' spoken language and their folklore. *The Dictionary of the Teton-Dakota Sioux* lists 30 words for the parts of a buffalo; 58 words for different kinds of grasses; and 145 names for flowers and weeds. Their mythology was also saturated with images from the natural world and populated with animals from the prairie.

Then, in the sixteenth century, European explorers appeared on the High Plains. They brought with them the horse, firearms, disease, and an alien culture. And nothing was ever again the same.

"Steam and electricity have not wrought a greater revolution in the ways of civilized life than the horse did in the savage life of the Plains," writes Walter Prescott Webb in *The Great Plains*. Webb suggests the horse enabled the Plains Indians to resist white domination longer than any other Indian group.

Although fossil remains show that a version of the horse evolved in North America, it had disappeared before the arrival of the Indians. When the horse reappeared carrying Spanish soldiers, the Indians were entranced. Soon they acquired their own through theft or by capturing strays.

The Kiowa and Missouri Indians were mounted by 1682, and soon the Pawnee, Comanche, Cree, Arikara, and other bands followed suit; within a century all the Plains Indians possessed horses. These Spanish horses, originally from North Africa, were bred for desert conditions and could thrive on the shortgrass without extensive grain feeding.

The Woodland Indians, hampered by forests, did not take to the horse with the same panache as did the Plains Indians, who made the mounted figure of an Indian wearing a warbonnet and war paint the symbol of all Indians in the popular imagination. With a horse to pull the travois, the Plains Indians traveled greater distances and became even better hunters and better warriors than before.

George Catlin, who visited the Plains Indians from 1832 to 1836, gave a vivid impression of these Indians both in his journals and in his paintings. He calls the Comanches "the most extraordinary horsemen that I have seen yet in all my travels" and describes one of the feats he witnessed:

He is able to drop his body upon the side of his horse at the instant he is passing, effectually screened from his enemies' weapons as he lies in a horizontal position behind the body of his horse, with his heels hanging over the horse's back; by which he has the power of throwing himself up again, and changing to the other side of the horse if necessary. In this wonderful condition, he will hang whilst his horse is at fullest speed, carrying with him his bow and his shield, and also his long lance of fourteen feet in length, all or either of which he will wield upon his enemy as he passes.

When the Plains Indians also acquired guns, they became a still more formidable foe. Even when limited to bow and arrow, some warriors were so skilled they could shoot fifteen to twenty arrows a minute and keep seven arrows in the air at once.

Skill, physical courage, and endurance were traits that defined Indian manhood and were necessary for survival on the prairie. "Counting coup" (literally meaning a "blow") was one measure of bravery. Most war deeds, such as taking a scalp or capturing ponies, counted as "coup." However, the greatest merit came from touching the enemy with the hand or a special "coup stick." The Indians considered touching an enemy a greater glory than merely killing without touch, and they painted such exploits on tepee covers or buffalo robes and recited the coup stories at tribal gatherings.

At the tribal gathering after the winter dispersal, warriors frequently performed dances that sometimes involved voluntary self-torture to prove their bravery. One of the most famous of these dances—the Sun Dance—centered around a man who allowed skewers and splints to be run through his breasts and fastened with cords to a center pole. The dancer leaned back so his weight hung from the "sacred tree" and slowly revolved around it staring fixedly at the sun for an entire day.

By 1780 the Plains Indian population was estimated at about 130,000. Intertribal warfare was quiescent, and the area seemed stable. Although the Indians had adopted the horse and the gun, their culture was otherwise little changed by the whites. Unfortunately, the horse and gun were not the only gifts "civilization" brought to the Indians.

In 1781 smallpox wiped out half their population. The disease spread quickly because of the nomadic lifestyle and the crowded summer camps and because the Indians had no concept of infection or contagion. The traditional method of treating sickness—a sweat bath followed by a plunge into a cold stream—added to the toll.

Trading parties and warring bands spread the pox.

Raiders took scalps from dying victims and plundered stricken camps, taking the disease, along with the booty, home with them. One Piegan survivor said, "We had no belief that one man could give it to another any more than a wounded man could give his wound to another."

The scourge returned again in the 1830s and destroyed the Mandan tribe. Out of a village of 1600 only 30 or 40 were left alive. Catlin says the few survivors were enslaved by the Arikara and some months later brought about their own death in a battle against the Sioux. "They wielded their weapons as desperately as they could to excite the fury of their enemy, and they were cut to pieces. . . . They are extinct."

Centuries of adapting to the High Plains could not prepare the Indians to cope with disease, whiskey, and other disasters brought on almost overnight by the whites. The clash of the two cultures and conflict over territory resulted in massacres, war, and injustice throughout the nineteenth century. Both sides committed atrocities as the Indians saw first the explorers, then a few covered wagons, then the railroad ("the black metal snake"), and finally hordes of settlers swarming over the land that had been free and open for as long as the rivers had run.

The Indians watched and, in the long run, were powerless to stop the homesteaders who "turned the land wrong side up." One Sioux warrior said, "The earth is our mother. One does not pound stakes in his mother." In *Land of the Spotted Eagle*, Luther Standing Bear wrote:

> We did not think of the great open plains, the beautiful rolling hills, and winding streams with tangled growth as "wild". . . . Not until the hairy man from the east came and with brutal frenzy heaped injustices upon us and the families we loved was it "wild" for us. When the very animals of the forest began fleeing from his approach, then it was that for us the 'Wild West' began.

The tragic story of the battles that ended the High Plains culture of the Indians and led to the reservation system is well known. Here we shall tell only the story of the Sand Creek Massacre.

During the 1860s Indian/white relations were badly strained throughout the Great Plains. Military attacks on Indians and unfair treaties foisted on them led to retaliation. Indians attacked some emigrant and freight trains and raided some outposts and farms. In June 1864, Colorado governor John Evans invited all Indians who wished to be considered "friendly" to report to the military authorities. Those who remained at large would be considered "hostile" and could be killed.

The Cheyennes led by Black Kettle and White Antelope and the Arapahos led by Little Raven and Left Hand accepted the peace invitation. Believing themselves under military protection, they set up camp at Sand Creek, thirty miles northeast of Fort Lyon. At dawn on November 29, 1864, Major John Chivington, leading a regiment composed mainly of unruly 100-day volunteers, mounted an unprovoked surprise attack against the Indians.

Chivington ordered his men to take "no prisoners," not even children, saying "nits make lice." Old men, women, and children were killed even as they tried to surrender, and their bodies were mutilated. Estimates of the dead ranged from 60 to 600. Even today no one knows how many actually died.

Years later George Bent, the half-blood son of Col. William Bent who ran Bent's Fort, retold the story of the carnage in his autobiography. Black Kettle's wife, who survived, was shot nine times as she lay wounded and helpless in the creekbed. Little Bear said that after the fight he returned and saw "even the wounded scalped and slashed. I saw one old woman wandering about; her whole scalp had been taken off and the blood was running down into her eyes so that she could not see where to go." Bent also reported that some of the soldiers cut skin from dead Cheyenne women to make tobacco bags.

Chief White Antelope, who had persuaded many of the Cheyennes to come to the camp, "decided to live no longer" when he saw the slaughter. With arms folded across his chest he stood in front of his lodge and sang the Indian death-song, which could also serve as a dirge for the passing of native American dominion over the plains:

Nothing lives long,
Only the earth and the mountains.

To the first non-Indian explorers, the prairie was unlike any land they had ever seen or dreamed of. They charted the way for the settlers, and they wrote journals and letters that described a place William Clark called "as butifull a peas of Land as ever I saw," and Edwin James called a land "of hopeless and ir-reclaimable sterility."

The discrepancies in the early accounts show how greatly individuals differ in their reaction to the plains. But the discrepancies also reflect how greatly the

Sandhills prairie at Sand Creek Massacre site: Chivington, Colorado

plains themselves change from season to season, from periodic drought years to wet years, and from riparian areas to the plateaus.

Coronado's expedition in 1541 was the first to experience the rigors of the shortgrass prairie. The Spanish pushed into Kansas on their quest for Quivira, the will-o'-the-wisp they sought after Cíbola turned out to be mud, not gold. But Coronado was not impressed with the poor village of Quivira and had the Indian who guided him there executed.

Castenada, who chronicled the expedition, complained that the land was so level, so featureless that it was necessary to mark the route with cow bones and dung. He wrote:

> Who could believe that 1000 horses and 500 of our cows and more than 5000 rams and ewes and more than 1500 friendly Indians and servants, in traveling over those plains, would leave no more trace where they had passed than if nothing had been there? . . . The grass never failed to become erect after it had been trodden down, and, although it was short, it was as fresh and straight as before.

Although no colonists followed the Conquistadors onto the High Plains, Coronado and other Spanish explorers left an important legacy: firearms and the horse.

For two and a half centuries after Coronado, the Great Plains remained "the Great Blank Space" on New World maps. Then within a few years fur trappers and traders and American explorers changed everything.

In 1803 the U.S. concluded the Louisiana Purchase, and a few months later Meriwether Lewis and William Clark embarked on their famous expedition. Some years earlier President Jefferson had tried unsuccessfully to initiate an expedition starting from Europe, crossing Russia and the Pacific Ocean, and proceeding across America from West to East. Walter Prescott Webb says such a laborious route showed "how formidable a trip overland . . . must have appeared at the time."

The Lewis and Clark expedition traveled mainly by water, so they saw little of the typical shortgrass prairie. In Montana, however, Sergeant Ordway called the country a desert and commented: "I do not conceive any part of it can ever be sitled as it is deficient of or in water except this River, of timber and too steep to be tilled." Clark admired the landscape, but even he complained of the aridity in Nebraska: "I am obliged to replinish my ink stand every day with fresh ink at least 9/10 of which must evaperate."

In 1806–1807 Zebulon Pike led a horseback party

across the central plains to search for the source of the Arkansas River. He compared "these vast plains" to the African desert and described "tracts of many leagues where the wind had thrown up the sand in all the fanciful forms of the ocean's rolling wave, and on which not a speck of vegetable matter existed."

Although Pike's chief mission was probably espionage (in fact, he was arrested and held briefly as a pampered "guest" of the Spanish in Santa Fe), he opened up new routes and added to the geographic knowledge of the plains. However, he also promoted the erroneous idea of the prairie as desert.

Stephen Long conducted the next major foray into the plains in 1819–1820, exploring the Platte and the Canadian rivers. Deserters stole most of the records of the trip except for the journals of Dr. Edwin James, who described the geology and natural history of the route. For several decades after Long mapped the area and coined the phrase "Great American Desert," his ideas influenced cartographers, who showed an emptiness labeled "Desert" between the Rockies and the Missouri.

Nicknamed "the Pathfinder," John Charles Frémont led five expeditions into the West, crossing the prairie and pioneering the Oregon Trail and others in the process. His *Narratives*, while somewhat exaggerated, paint an exciting picture of the region and show the ingenuity needed by early explorers. For instance, on an early trip with the French scientist Nicollet, Frémont repaired a barometer by replacing the broken glass with a buffalo horn scraped thin and bent into a tube.

Food was always a major concern for the explorers, though game was usually plentiful and could be cooked over a fire made from "bois de vache," or cow dung. Frémont's description of two feasts shows cultural differences in what is considered "gourmet." On one occasion the whites served a pot-au-feu to a group of Indian chiefs. "With the first mouthful each Indian silently laid down his spoon and looked at each other." Swiss cheese had been added to the stew, and "until this strange flavor was accounted for the Indians thought they were being poisoned." Another time the Indians honored the explorers with a dog feast. As a special mark of favor an Indian would sometimes kill his favorite dog for such an occasion. To refuse to eat it would be an insult. The meat, Frémont said, tasted like glutinous mutton.

In spite of the dangers and hardships, many of the explorers exulted in the beauty of the wilderness. "Indians and buffalo make the poetry and life of the prairie," wrote Frémont, "and our camp was full of their exhilaration."

These were the most famous expeditions to cross

Left—
Plains Indian campsite in
Picture Canyon: Comanche
National Grassland, Colorado

Oregon Trail ruts:
Guernsey, Wyoming

the prairies, but there were many more: soldiers establishing forts, surveyors staking out railroad routes, and wealthy men such as Prince Maximilian, the German naturalist, and Sir William Drummond Stewart, the Scottish laird and sportsman. Many of these expeditions brought along scientists and artists, including Thomas Say, Thomas Nuttall, George Catlin, Carl Bodmer, and Alfred Jacob Miller to record a disappearing culture and landscape.

As the explorers opened up the country and made traveling easier, gentleman adventurers, such as Francis Parkman and Mark Twain, came to record their impressions of a "sun-scorched landscape" that could also produce fatal winter blizzards. Although Parkman described the prairie as "dreary and monotonous," he also wrote, "yet the wild beasts and wild men that frequent the valley of the Platte make it a scene of interest and excitement to the traveler. Of those who have journeyed there, scarcely one, perhaps, fails to look back with fond regret to his horse and rifle."

Parkman spent several months crossing the prairies in 1846. In the 1860s Mark Twain took six days to journey from St. Louis to Fort Kearny (300 miles) by stage coach. Within a decade the transcontinental railroad was complete, and Twain wrote in astonishment that the same 300-mile trek could now be done in fifteen hours and forty minutes.

By the mid-1800s emigrants, almost as thick as the buffalo once had been, surged along trails heading for Oregon, California, New Mexico, or Utah. Five-foot-deep ruts can still be seen in areas where the Oregon Trail crossed the plains. No longer did the grass spring up "as fresh and straight as before," and the Indians watched in consternation, knowing these hordes were a portent of more to come.

Most emigrants stopped in the plains only long enough to bury their dead in shallow graves marked by a pile of stones—if even stones could be found. The trails were also marked by precious belongings discarded when the remaining oxen or mules could no longer pull the heavy loads. Those who came after might find scattered bones, a child's beloved doll, an inlaid wardrobe, a violin, or a piano beside the trail.

The Mormons, forced from their homes by often violent prejudice, were especially ill-equipped to survive the plains. In 1846 at "Winter Quarters" in Nebraska, more than 600 died. Afterwards, in the language of the prairies, "Mormon winter" came to mean the first terrible winter faced by new settlers. In 1855, when the church ran short of money for wagons, Brigham Young ordered handcarts built. It took four people to push and pull one of these heavy, two-wheeled carts across the High Plains, the rivers, and the mountains to reach the promised land.

Although the trip across the plains was grueling, many westering pioneers looked out on the prairies and saw the beauty and felt a sadness for a way of life they were displacing. Martha Maxwell, who crossed the plains in a covered wagon in 1860 and later became one of the first women naturalists, wrote: "Houses are getting quite common, nearly every patch of firtle bottomland is fenced or about to be. This I think is not right for it must interfere very much with the Indians depriving them of their hunting ground and particularly of pastarage for their ponys."

After the Homestead Act was passed in 1862, throngs of people came to stake a claim. During the ensuing years, many failed and were quick to shake the prairie dust from their heels as they returned to the East. But, always, a few stayed on.

The ones who stayed and put down roots on the shortgrass prairie learned to grow their crops and to build their homes with little water and practically no wood. They also learned to endure hardships and horrors that make the tall tales told around campfires seem almost tame. Today we read of a lone pioneer woman nursing her four children and her husband through a plague and burying them one by one

Register Cliffs:
Guernsey, Wyoming

Left—
Sod house:
Toadstool Park, Nebraska

in a shallow prairie grave, or of a farmer starting all over again when locusts destroyed his crops for the third year in a row—and we wonder how they could do it.

Folklorist Roger Welsch once asked that question of an old-timer, who replied, "Perhaps it was like the dog that shinnied up a tree when a bobcat was hot on his tail: he didn't climb that tree because he could, but rather because he had to."

The first thing the settlers had to do was build a place to live, and that place was usually a dugout or a soddy. The dugout was a cave dug into a hill or the side of an arroyo. It was damp, dark, and dirty but well insulated from heat, cold, and wind. Its biggest drawback was obvious when it rained. In *Pioneer Women*, Joanna Stratton quotes a Kansas woman who wrote, "After the storms, we carried the water out with buckets, then waded around in the mud until it dried up. Then, to keep us nerved up, the bull snakes would get in the roof and now and then one would lose his hold and fall down on the bed." There were even stories of buffalo and livestock falling through the roof.

Except for a stovepipe or sod chimney, the dugout was usually level with the prairie and difficult for a wayfarer to find. Frequently travelers thought they were crossing uninhabited terrain until they saw a pipe sticking out of the ground.

When the prairie was so uniformly flat that home builders could find no hill for a dugout, they built a house of sod and called it "prairie marble." They laid the sod blocks grass side down to a thickness of about two feet; spanned the outside walls with a framework of willow brush or poles; and roofed it with more sod, grass side up. Mark Twain wrote, "It was the first time we had ever seen a man's front yard on top of his house."

According to Joanna Stratton, the builders needed one acre of prairie turf to build a one-room sod house measuring sixteen by twenty feet and weighing about ninety tons. And of course they used no mortar or nails. Some women brightened their soddies by whitewashing the inside walls and planting wild verbena and prickly pear on the roof. Like the dugout, the soddy was sodden when it rained and dusty when it didn't. But it did provide more space, and it was above ground.

The settlers learned to use prairie products to survive. When the buffalo became scarce, they fished and hunted deer, antelope, rabbits, ducks, geese, grouse, and prairie chickens, and the Indians taught them how to preserve the meat by making pemmican and jerky. They cooked over fires made from buffalo or cattle chips or twists of hay. They used animal fat to fry food, make candles and lye soap, waterproof boots, and grease paper to cover the window holes.

They gathered wild fruits and early spring greens such as lamb's quarters or dandelions. They made vinegar from wild plums, grapes, or melon and tea from rose hips, mint, and mullen. Sometimes they lived all winter on just corn mush and beans, and even calling beans "prairie strawberries" didn't vary the taste. But sometimes they feasted on tender prairie chicken flavored with wild garlic and washed down with wild currant wine.

Usually they spun their own yarn and wove their own cloth. Sometimes they dyed the cloth using goldenrod or onion skins for yellow, marigolds for orange, choke cherries for purple, and the cochineal beetle that lives on the prickly pear for red.

Most wood had to be shipped in and was expensive, if available at all. In 1860 Martha Maxwell wrote that one stick four or five inches wide by five or six feet long sold for fifty cents—pretty costly for fence posts. And fencing was essential if farmers wanted to prevent livestock from trampling their fields.

In western Kansas farmers discovered that limestone worked as well as wood for fence posts. They drilled holes in the rock, drove in wedges, and split off a block just the right size for a fence post. When freshly quarried, the stone was soft enough to be sawed,

notched, or drilled, but it quickly hardened into fence posts as serviceable as wooden ones. In the 1870s a stone post cost only twenty-five cents, including delivery. These posts, weighing some 350 pounds each, were set out at a rate of about 170 posts per mile. Many still stand along Interstate 70.

In addition to making do with limited natural resources, the settlers suffered from conflicts with unfriendly Indians and cattlemen. They also had to endure an unforgiving climate.

John Wesley Powell, who wrote "Report on the Land of the Arid Regions of the U.S." in 1878, eventually adopted the term "sub-humid" for this region because so many people objected to the term "arid." But "arid" was the right word, as many pioneers discovered. Tree ring studies indicate droughts recur in approximately twenty-two-year cycles that may be related to sunspot activity. Farmers would enjoy several moist years before hitting the bad ones. The 1896 *Yearbook* of the Department of Agriculture describes such a year:

The grasses wither, the herds wander wearily over the plains in search of water holes, the crops wilt and languish, yielding not even the seed for another year. . . . The settlers depart with such of their household furniture as can be drawn away by the enfeebled draft

Stone fence posts:
western Kansas

animals, the herds disappear, and this beautiful land, once so fruitful, is now dry and brown and given over to the prairie wolf.

After a drought in 1860, Kansas lost a third of its population. As usual, those who persevered did so with a grim sort of humor. According to Roger Welsch, it got so dry one year that two cottonwoods were seen fighting over a dog. And it got so hot that the corn began popping as it was planted; the cane melted, ran down the hill into the corn and made popcorn balls, which the farmer sold for five cents each.

Along with the heat and drought came wind. The wind drove some pioneer women mad, and the longing "for something to hide behind" was almost universal. The parching wind could dry up crops in a matter of hours. Joanna Stratton tells of one pioneer woman who remembered the cornfields on a golden Sunday: "It was like a garden, not a weed to be seen and all in the tassel. . . . Then came a hot wind and by sundown that corn wasn't worth cutting. Grasp a handful of leaves and you could powder it all up in your hand almost like charred paper."

Often the wind came in the funnel-shape of a tornado that could flatten a farm in seconds and send families scurrying for the cyclone cellar. The highest

surface wind velocity ever recorded was in a tornado at Wichita Falls, Texas, where the wind reached 280 miles per hour. A capricious tornado could reduce one house to rubble and leave the next untouched. According to tall-tale teller Welsch, it could uproot an oak, deposit it on a barn two miles away, and not disturb one egg or fledgling in the twenty nests in its branches.

If searing drought and wind didn't get the crops, hail frequently did. And then there were the locusts that hit the roofs so hard they sounded like hail. In *Sod and Stubble* John Ise describes a grasshopper invasion:

> Like a cloud of glistening snow flakes it was, but the flakes were alive, eddying and whirling about like the wild, dead leaves in an autumn storm; and soon the flakes came down, circling in myriads, beating against everything animate or inanimate. Grasshoppers — millions, billions of them — soon covered the ground in a seething, fluttering mass, their jaws constantly at work.

They consumed everything: crops, clothing, curtains, harnesses, anything that absorbed sweat. One day a Kansas woman wore a white dress with a green stripe, according to Joanna Stratton. Grasshoppers settled on her and ate the green stripe from her dress. Tracks became so slick from crushed grasshoppers that trains could not run. Bonfires built to kill the pests were actually smothered by them. This plague returned, in varying degrees of severity, year after year.

Winter brought no respite from calamity. Killing blizzards came without warning. Mari Sandoz writes of a blizzard called "the schoolchildren's storm" because so many died in it. It happened on January 12, 1888, just as children were leaving school. In some cases teachers kept the children at school or tied them together and led them to safety. One group never made it across the 200 yards to a boarding house. Altogether more than 200 people were killed.

Western movies and novels have played up the horror of bloody Indian raids against helpless outposts of whites. Although such raids were comparatively rare, one did take place on June 11, 1864, on the isolated Hungate farm east of Denver. A small band of Indians descended on the lone wife and her two children, killing them all and setting fire to the house. Seeing the flames, Mr. Hungate rushed home and was also killed. Later the bodies were taken to Denver and displayed to public view. This incident inflamed public opinion and was one factor leading to the Sand Creek Massacre.

Just as the movies exaggerated the savagery of the Indians, they romanticized the cattlemen who dominated the prairie scene for about twenty years from the 1860s to the late 1880s. This was the time of the great cattle drives from Texas to the northern ranges and to the railroads. Their routes, such as the Goodnight-Loving Trail, can still be traced on the prairies today.

In 1871 cowboys drove some 700,000 cattle up from Texas. Robert Ferris calls that the "peak year" for the cattle barons and tells about the day a thunderstorm stampeded eleven herds totaling about 30,000 Longhorns. It took 120 cowboys ten days to unscramble them.

Enmity grew between the cattlemen whose livestock rampaged across the farmers' fields, and the farmers, who fenced off what had once been open range. Some ranchers hired gunmen to kill homesteaders brazen enough to shoot cattle destroying their crops. One child was shot at just for shooing the cows away. Two cattlemen named Print and Bob Olive were especially notorious for their lynching parties against farmers, and they earned Nebraska the epithet "Man-Burner State." In 1877 they hanged two homesteaders, doused their bodies with coal oil, and burned them. So terrorized was the community that no one dared take down the bodies for several days.

After each bloody conflict or natural disaster, some

families would leave, and the slogan "In God we trusted, in Kansas we busted" became a cliché. The settlers lampooned the Homestead Act, calling it a case where the government was willing to bet the homesteader 160 acres that he would starve to death on it in less than five years, the amount of time allowed to "prove up" the claim. Later the acreage allotted under the Act was increased to 320, but even that was inadequate for eking out a living on the inhospitable plains. According to Welsch, some of those who hung on made up a song that ended: "We do not live we only stay, 'cause we're too poor to move away."

Poor, and lonely. That was the fate of many settlers. It took courage to face the dangers of tornadoes, blizzards, and Indians, but, as one of Joanna Stratton's women said, it took even more courage "to live twenty-four hours at a time, month in and month out, on the lonely and lovely prairie, without giving up to the loneliness."

The Kansas painter John Noble likened the feeling to a disease:

You look on, on, on, out into space, out almost beyond time itself. You see nothing but the rise and swell of land and grass, and then more grass—the monotonous, endless prairie! A stranger traveling on the prairie would get his hopes up, expecting to see something different on making the next rise. To him the disappointment and monotony were terrible. "He's got loneliness," we would say of such a man.

Ole Rolvaag focused *Giants in the Earth* on the loneliness of his heroine and on "the strange spell of sadness which the unbroken solitude cast upon the minds of some. . . . It is hard for the eye to wander from skyline to skyline, year in and year out, without finding a resting place!"

But just as the bleak prairie produces glorious wildflowers, sunrises, and sunsets, the lonely life of the pioneer was often lit with humor, diversion, and a deep attachment to the land. Roger Welsch's tall tales show the homesteaders laughing at adversity. House raisings, harvestings, and quilting bees were turned into festive occasions. The settlers also enjoyed church socials, picnics, and square dancing. Caller Gib Gilbert says that until recently the dances were often called "play parties" so strict churchgoers who disapproved of dancing could do-si-do with a clear conscience.

By the late nineteenth century several innovations were making life easier for the settlers. Historians agree that two inventions finally enabled many determined homesteaders to succeed: barbed wire and

Left —
Windmill: Pawnee National
Grassland, Colorado

the windmill.

Today barbed wire is so common we snicker on hearing that a museum has actually collected 500 different kinds. But this twist of metal helped resolve the range wars in the homesteader's favor. It was cheap and effective, and soon it fenced in both cattle and crops. In the long run, ranchers also benefited. Fencing enabled them to raise blooded stock, isolated from the less desirable native cattle.

The windmill, which brought water to an arid land, has become the symbol of the prairie, the sign of human habitation. Sometimes it's the only structure that breaks the horizontal lines of land and sky. Like barbed wire, it was cheap and effective. Railroaders, ranchers, and farmers used it to harness the usually cursed wind for engines, cows, and corn. Soon every lone farmhouse had its windmill, and because of the windmill, the houses proliferated.

The Industrial Revolution during the latter part of the nineteenth century led to greater and cheaper production of windmills, well drills, grain drills, and tractors. It also produced the steel plows that broke the plains. John Deere's new invention was a revolutionary change from the buffalo shoulder blade used by the Indians or the tree dragged by oxen that was used by some poverty-stricken "nesters." Farmers developed irrigation and "dry farming" (using special methods of tillage to conserve soil moisture) and were so successful that plainsmen began to scoff at the notion of "the Great American Desert."

The scoffing stopped when the black blizzards of the 1930s started. Almost a century earlier the Indians had warned, "Grass no good upside down." But the sodbusters arrived to find fertile soil that needed no clearing—and they quickly turned it over.

Lawrence Svobida arrived in Meade County, Kansas, in 1929 and attacked the land with vigor: "My tractor roared day and night," he wrote about his first year. "I had a man driving from six in the morning until six in the evening. Then I would drive throughout the entire night." He told his story in *Farming the Dust Bowl* after he left the region following seven wheat crop failures in eight years—his heart and health as broken as the land.

The drought of the 1930s persisted for most of that decade. "Too frequent plowing pulverized the soil to dust so fine it resembled ashes," wrote Svobida. And in 1932 the powder-dry soil, no longer held back by grass, started to blow.

The dust storms, moving at a velocity of forty to fifty miles per hour, blotted out the sun. Lights had to be turned on at noon. On May 11, 1934, one storm blew an estimated 300,000,000 tons of topsoil from the plains. Mrs. Reul Bowman, a rancher's wife who survived the Dust Bowl in eastern Colorado, remembers fences completely buried in blowing dust. Then more fences were built on top of fences, sometimes three fences deep. David Costello tells of finding a nest built by a desperate crow who, unable to find twigs, used pieces of barbed wire.

Dirt clogged the engines of cars, tractors, and trains. Roads and railroads were buried. Svobida said the accumulation of dirt was more than the snowplows could handle; it had to be hand shoveled from roads and out of houses. Birds, jack rabbits, and cattle suffocated. The Red Cross set up emergency hospitals. Many people wore goggles and face masks. And some died, their lungs filled with dust.

Year after year the wheat died as well—if it came up at all. Federal agencies created by President Franklin D. Roosevelt tried to help. The National Industrial Recovery Act of 1933 and later the Emergency Relief Appropriations Act allowed the government to buy the worst of the "blowout areas" for fifty cents to eight dollars an acre and to relocate the farmers to more favorable areas. The ruined farms, which became known as the Land Utilization Projects, were reseeded with grass. Historian Donald Worster says ten thousand houses were abandoned on the High Plains and nine million acres of farmland were turned back to nature.

During this period storms sometimes carried dirt from the plains clear across the country to settle on ships 300 miles offshore in the Atlantic Ocean. One day in 1935 hearings were being held in Washington, D.C. on a bill to establish the Soil Conservation Service. A shadow passed over the hearing room, and one senator said, "It's getting dark."

Hugh Bennet, nicknamed the "Father of Soil Conservation," was testifying for the bill. He thundered: "There, gentlemen, goes Oklahoma!"

The Soil Conservation Bill passed, and the Soil Conservation Service taught farmers modern methods of agriculture such as strip cropping and contour plowing. They built terraces and windbreaks and introduced more drought-resistant grains. The Agricultural Adjustment Administration, another agency created by Roosevelt, saved many farmers from bankruptcy by paying them to allow part of the land to lie fallow, reducing production of surplus crops.

Some of these programs succeeded so well that by the end of the 1940s sand dunes had been rehabilitated into cornfields. However, Donald Worster claims in *The Dust Bowl* that New Deal conservation on the Great Plains was, on balance, a failure because it did not fundamentally change American attitudes of materialism or promote what ecologist Aldo Leopold called "the conservation ethic."

Worster says we still depend on technological fixes, such as center-pivot irrigation, and disregard the long-term effects of our actions. Instead of facing up to the limits of our natural resources, we prefer to expand production, planting crops "from fence row to fence row." Worster once asked a farm woman what would happen when the irrigation water ran out. "I don't think that in our time it can," she replied. "And if it does we'll get more from someplace else. The Lord never intended for us to do without water."

Despite its failings, the New Deal did set in motion several enlightened programs that still serve as models today. For instance, in 1960 the Secretary of Agriculture created nineteen national grasslands, some of which are shortgrass prairie, from the former Land Utilization Projects. "Our goal was to stabilize the economy and to re-establish native habitat," said the late Steward Adams, head ranger at Pawnee National Grassland for twelve years. "As the habitat was re-established, wildlife started to come back. The mountain plover, which left when the shortgrass disappeared, came back when the grass came back."

CHAPTER FIVE

> Prairie is much more than land covered with grass. It is a slowly evolved, highly complex organic entity, centuries old. . . . Once destroyed it can never be replaced by man.
>
> —J. E. Weaver,
> *The North American Prairie*

Footsteps Present

Today many people have forgotten the Dust Bowl. The Army runs tanks on a fragile prairie in southeastern Colorado. Suburbia swallows large chunks each year. Aquifers are being depleted at an alarming rate. Some farmers destroy wetlands and put every available acre into production. Some ranchers run too many cattle on too little land, and others fail to pay fair market value for grazing fees on public lands. The subtitle of a 1986 congressional report sums it up: "All Is Not Well on the Range."

But there are others who remember what happened when the grass disappeared. These people—ranchers, rangers, researchers, and people who just plain like open spaces—are working to keep the prairie healthy.

It would be hard to find a prettier prairie, for instance, than the 28,000 acre Lasater ranch near Matheson, Colorado. The cattle grazing on the lush range are "gentled" to the point that they will eat from a stranger's hand. However, Tom Lasater and his son Dale, who raise their famous Beefmaster breed, might themselves be considered mavericks.

Left—
Winter wheat field: Oglala
National Grassland, Nebraska

Tom originated the breed (a cross of Hereford, Shorthorn, and Brahman) in 1931 and moved from Texas to Colorado in 1948. "When we moved up here we decided to turn everything back to nature. Nature's smarter than all of us put together," he says. "So we stepped back out of the way and let nature take over. . . . We don't kill cactus; we don't kill nothing." They allow no poisoning, no shooting, and no trapping. The Lasaters have designated their ranch a wildlife sanctuary and are proud that healthy forage grasses have crowded out most of the undesirable species, and that coyotes and cattle manage to coexist.

The success of the Lasater method is obvious, and delegations have come from China and from Australia to observe. Bottomland that Dale remembers as nothing but sand when he was a child out hunting arrowheads is now covered with grass, and groves of cottonwoods line Big Sandy Creek. Fifty-two species of birds were counted here in a four-hour period a few years ago, and deer and antelope roam in peace.

Recently Dale started using Allan Savory's methods, with some modifications, to improve the rangeland. Savory originated the controversial theory that you can actually graze more cattle on "brittle environments" with less damage if you move the cattle frequently to different pastures at the proper time. He compares this grazing pattern to that of the buffalo, which grazed an area intensively for a short time, aerating it with their hooves, and then moved on, not to return until the grass recovered.

When grass is growing fast, the cattle are moved before they can take what Dale calls "the second bite." It's that second severe bite just as the grass starts to grow again that causes the plant to lose root capacity and eventually depletes the choice, or "ice-cream," grasses, according to Savory. Dale is making two major changes on the ranch to reflect these ideas: "We're not using exactly the same place at exactly the same time of the growing season every year . . . and we're putting in electric fences and moving cattle through a series of paddocks."

Brian Sindelar, Professor of Range Sciences at Montana State University, has served as a board member for the Center for Holistic Resource Management since 1978 and has conducted several research projects on the mechanisms involved in the system. "I believe very strongly that it is the only bright ray of hope at present for agriculture, conservation, and biological education," he says. Most of the problems he encounters are associated with human foibles. "People recently acquainted with HRM, and especially with minimal training in HRM, are generally quite excited about the model and are in a great rush to use it," he says, but "they may fail to carefully watch where they're going and what they're doing. That's dangerous."

Critics of the Savory approach say it would be expensive to manage properly and would result in even greater overgrazing than at present. They fear most ranchers will not be as careful as Dale Lasater. Because Savory's ideas, which were developed in Africa, are relatively new to the U.S., no one knows how they will work over a long period of time. Range consultant Jon Skovlin recently returned from three years of consulting in sub-Sahara Africa. In the August 1987 issue of *Rangelands* he claims that studies in southern Africa show that the method is not working: "Evidence in literature from Zimbabwe and elsewhere in southern Africa indicates that it is impossible to have both heavy stocking and improvement in range condition."

Steve Johnson, Southwest representative for Defenders of Wildlife, compares Holistic Resource Management to the Ghost Dance that many Indians in the late 1800s hoped would bring back the grass and the buffalo. But writer Sam Bingham and others who have worked with the HRM model claim that Savory's ideas, along with other good ranching practices, will help redeem our abused rangelands.

Another rancher who loves and protects the prairie is Willard Louden, who runs cattle on 30,000 acres near the Mesa de Maya in southeastern Colorado. More than a rancher, Louden is also a landscape painter and an archaeologist. He leads nature classes for children and adults, produces wildlife movies, has served in the Peace Corps and on the board of The Nature Conservancy, and belongs to a dozen or so conservation organizations.

He also had the guts to do battle with the Army. In the early 1980s, Fort Carson decided to take over nearly 250,000 acres of public and private land in Las Animas and Baca counties for Army maneuvers. According to an Army officer, this area was chosen because it was considered especially "challenging" for the division's tanks and other vehicles.

"There's no way you can run a tank around, do a 360 degree turn, and not tear up a whole bunch of blue grama," says Louden, who spearheaded the fight to stop the Army from taking over the land, which included part of the Comanche National Grassland.

Louden and a coalition of ranchers and conservationists lost the battle but did manage to wring a few concessions on land use from the Army. And perhaps he showed the way to a future where ranchers and conservationists will work together for the good of the land. Most ranchers, he says, are doing their best to foster a healthy prairie. He sees hope for prairie preservation if we can pull together knowledge from both botanists and on-site ranchers, "if we can learn what practices are good . . . and get some concerted effort to see the land not only maintained, but rejuvenated." He also believes it will be necessary to get financial support so ranchers can afford to follow the best environmental practices. "We could sell off and live better off the income than we've ever lived in our lives, but we don't want to do that," he says. "We like what we're doing, we're happy here, we feel that we are constructive, productive members of society. I think that's what we need to strive for."

We asked everyone we talked to, "What is the chief problem facing prairies today?" and almost always the answer was "People, of course." Betsy Webb, Curator of Zoology at the Denver Museum of Natural History, says "Conversion to cropland, overgrazing by cattle, and human settlement patterns are the three big ones."

In 1986 Representative Mike Synar of Oklahoma chaired a subcommittee that investigated the problems arising from grazing on public lands. Their findings were published in a report titled *Federal Grazing Program: All is Not Well On the Range*. They found that just 2 percent of the country's livestock producers are allotted permits to graze stock on the public lands administered by the Bureau of Land Management and the Forest Service. The 23,000 permittees pay only $1.54 per animal unit month whereas on the open market they would pay an average of $6.87 on nonfederal lands or $6.53 on federal lands. These low grazing fees covered only about 35 percent of the costs of administering the program. The committee also discovered that some permittees sublease BLM land for "windfall profits."

Included in the report was a short section labeled "Damage to the Land—Competing Uses Shortchanged." According to environmental impact statements prepared by the BLM itself, 71 percent of their rangeland is in "unsatisfactory" condition. The Forest Service rangeland is in somewhat better shape, although some of their allotments were also judged unsatisfactory.

Perhaps we need a program that would help all ranchers, not just the privileged 2 percent, and at the same time help restore the prairie. The Lasaters, the Loudens, and many others believe properly managed livestock ranching and a flourishing prairie can be compatible. In fact, Earl Johnson, who was president of the Pawnee Grazing Association for thirty-one years, says, "If it isn't grazed, it will deteriorate. The less you graze it, the more old grass you get."

Although that statement provokes controversy among some ecologists, research scientist David Schimel agrees and says, "I think anyone who thinks they can manage a grassland reserve by eliminating grazing is fooling themselves. . . . Ecology is starting to recognize that certain types of disturbance (fire, grazing, possibly even drought and storms) are part of the maintenance of an ecosystem. Old grazing enclosures in the Pawnee have been studied by the U.S.D.A. for many years. Almost without exception those enclosures have been invaded by exotic weeds. Both extremes—overgrazing and no grazing—have similar effects." Ecologist Durward Allen adds that "On the early plains, buffalo wallowing and trekking were important disturbance factors."

Earl Johnson also points out that ranchers with grazing permits must agree to certain restrictions on the use of their own land and are responsible for the upkeep of improvements such as windmills and water tanks. He remembers the Dust Bowl and the beginnings of federal farm aid that led to the Grasslands program. "This was a bad mess," he says. "People were not able to make a living here farming . . . and when the government stepped in and bought all that land, I think it's one of the best things that ever happened."

Many people still try to farm marginal land. Not far from where Johnson lives, a Canadian specula-

Lesser yellowlegs at sunset: Boulder County, Colorado

tor created a tempest in 1982 when he attempted to plow 16,000 acres of dry grassland. He hoped to increase land value by converting pastureland to cropland, but the local people remembered the dust storms all too well. Not the dust storms of the 1930s, but the ones that hit farmland in the 1950s and again in the 1970s.

Doris McDonnell was one of many who called for a moratorium on the plowing. She described the dust storms of the fifties in an article in *The Denver Post*:

We live in Hugo, having come here from Byers over 20 years ago. The thing that amazed me when we first came here was that whenever I talked . . . about the drought in 1955 and '56 and '57, they didn't know what I was talking about. . . . It finally dawned on me, "Of course not, this is grazing land." In their towns they hadn't seen their whole world disappear like ours in Byers did. They didn't have to turn on their lights in the daytime when the skies would suddenly become as dark as the night. Or stuff their windows with wet towels to try to keep the sifting dust out of their houses. . . . The vacuum cleaners would quit working because the fine dust would get into the mechanisms. A wet mop would soon be filled with mud."

The public outcry resulted in a temporary moratorium on plowing. The speculator sold his land. And Weld County instituted regulations prohibiting anyone in the future from breaking sod without a permit.

But in other parts of the prairie, farmers continue to bust the sod, causing a loss of topsoil estimated by some to be greater than during the Dust Bowl. In Colorado alone 738,923 acres of fragile grasslands were plowed between 1978 and 1987.

At the same time, pumpage irrigation for both farms and towns is draining underlying aquifers. Water levels in the Ogallala Aquifer that underlies much of the shortgrass prairie are declining at the rate of one half to two and one half feet per year (depending on the location) according to a 1983 report issued by the Resource Analysis Section, Colorado Department of Agriculture. One million acre feet are pumped from Colorado each year with only 430,000 acre feet being replenished. If we continue at present rates, the report predicts that the Ogallala Aquifer will be virtually gone by the year 2060.

Hydrologist John B. Weeks, who heads an eight-state project to study the aquifers of the High Plains, says the largest water level drop documented by the U.S. Geological Survey was from one well in Floyd County, Texas, that fell 200 feet from 1940 to 1980, an average of five feet per year. Although the ground water level appears to have stabilized during the past couple of years, the improvement may be only a temporary one caused by high energy prices and low crop prices, factors that affect the amount of water farmers can afford to pump.

The 1985 Food and Security Act, frequently called the "Sodbuster Act," may give renewed hope to an abused land. This legislation denies federal subsidies to farmers who bring new, highly erodible lands (including wetlands) into production. The law also provides for a "conservation reserve" fund to pay farmers to plant marginal land with grasses or trees and to remove them from crop production for at least ten years. In 1986 the U.S. Department of Agriculture enrolled almost 9 million acres in this program. In Colorado 333,152 acres have been reseeded, and other states with shortgrass prairie are carrying out similar restorations.

Taking land out of production is one answer to the problem of erosion. Wes Jackson, co-director with his wife Dana of the Land Institute in Salina, Kansas, has turned the problem upside-down and envisions an unusual solution. In *New Roots for American Agriculture*, he proposes using perennial grain crops as an alternative to corn and wheat on semiarid or erosion-prone land. Researchers are trying to develop a hardy, high-protein perennial grain which, Jackson believes, would benefit marginal lands.

Once the prairie sod has been turned over for farming or suburbia, it's a Herculean task to restore it. After the Dust Bowl, Earl Johnson reseeded his land, experimenting with different types of exotic grasses such as crested wheat and Russian rye. He also set one fifty-acre plot aside. "I just slowly let nature take care of it, and nature has got it all covered up with buffalo and grama."

Horticulturist Richard Brune is also trying to restore prairie on a few acres at the Denver Botanic Gardens. But, he says, "It took 10,000 years to make a prairie—you're not going to restore it in three or ten or even one hundred years." Brune, whose goal is to re-create a microcosm of the prairie "the way it was when the first explorers saw it," has established examples of sandhill, midgrass, and tallgrass prairies as well as shortgrass.

Brune gave up a job in analytical chemistry to take on this difficult and low-paying job. What made the project so vital? "It's important for people to appreciate the prairie as something to enjoy other than just driving through it to reach the mountains," he says. "It's of economic value. There's lots of plant material whose value is unknown which could be of importance for the gene pool. It's habitat for wildlife. It's appropriate for the climate and resistant to weeds. It's hard for exotics to invade a healthy prairie." He hopes that after seeing a "backyard" type prairie, others will try out some of the ideas such as using buffalo grass instead of bluegrass for lawns.

Not everyone appreciates a restored prairie, however. Richard Brune once overheard a visitor say, "This looks just like a vacant lot!" Since then several thousand additional plants, including eighty-seven new species of wildflowers, have been added, but education is needed to enable most people to really "see" a prairie.

One organization that fosters prairie appreciation is the Plains Conservation Center east of Aurora, Colorado. A director, two caretakers, and a group of enthusiastic volunteers keep the center and 2000 acres of shortgrass prairie going. They also lead field trips for schools and schedule special events such as the "Pioneer Village Open House," where a "mountain man" spins yarns, "pioneer women" spin wool, a blacksmith forges iron, and everyone has a good time while learning what life was like in the soddies.

About 6500 people a year visit the center and learn what a prairie is like. Volunteer Elizabeth Watson sums up why the center is so important: "I see houses eating up the land, and it's sad. We have to have open space. Once it's gone, it's gone forever. You don't realize the noise in the city till you get out on the prairie. Here you can see the stars and hear the coyote."

Ed Butterfield helps people see the prairie in depth

through the Grassland Institute, a week-long seminar he has directed for thirteen years. Sponsored by the Denver Audubon Society, the Institute is held every June at Pawnee National Grassland in Colorado. The participants not only listen to talks given by ranchers, range specialists, and university professors, but they also get out on their hands and knees to discover what makes a prairie. They learn to run transects to determine plant density; they collect and identify insects; and they take field trips to the diverse habitats encompassed by the Grassland.

At the end of a week of intense learning the participants agree that just as the prairie is more diverse than it appears at first sight, the problems are more complex than they appear. Usually consensus is reached on just one issue: there is need for more research, for more baseline data. "Do I have all the answers?" asks Kim Carroll, who directs reclamation at the largest open pit mine in North America (Black Thunder Mine on Thunder Basin National Grassland in Wyoming). "I don't even have all the questions!"

Perhaps the most important research group asking and answering questions about the shortgrass prairie today is the "Long-Term Ecological Research Program" sponsored by the National Science Foundation. Their goal is to study a variety of ecosystems including forests, wetlands, prairies, and deserts. One tar-

geted site is the shortgrass prairie at the Central Plains Experimental Range where researchers from Colorado State University and the Department of Agriculture are working jointly to determine the long-term effects of climate, soils, grazing management, and other types of disturbances.

"This program follows approximately forty years of research at the Central Plains Experimental Range," says Bill Lauenroth, principal investigator for the program. "We hope to get a basis for long-term verification or rejection of the current collection of ideas we use to manage the region. Over decades we expect to give these ideas a thorough testing."

Knowledge derived from this program will help revegetation and recovery efforts following disturbances. Lauenroth envisions a reversal of the practice of plowing marginal lands in the shortgrass region and says, "In the next decades we hope to understand better how to put lands that were plowed in the seventies back into grassland. . . . In the next cycle of drought these sites will need to be put back into permanent vegetation."

The Botanic Gardens restoration, the Plains Conservation Center, the National Grasslands, and similar units throughout the Great Plains are impressive. But many people believe we need more than "museum" prairies or grazing lands.

However, in order to preserve authentic prairie, first you must find it. Some of the best sleuths looking for prairies and other places worth saving are connected with the Colorado Natural Areas Program. More than thirty states have similar programs that work with local landowners, both private and government. They inventory unique natural areas that should be protected and make land management recommendations regarding them.

Sue Galatowitsch, an ecologist with the Colorado Natural Areas Program, studies the literature to discover what species of plants existed during presettlement days in order to develop a "search image." Then she visits prospective sites and flies over them looking for prairie remnants. She says it's hard to develop a profile on shortgrass prairie because nearly all of it has been heavily grazed: "It's hard to tell what a prairie would have looked like when it was grazed by bison and not by cows." Galatowitsch describes the shortgrass prairie as "a mosaic" and says that because of grazing, "It's probably become less of a mosaic and more homogenous." This controversy over just what makes a high-quality shortgrass prairie has been a stumbling block in establishing preserves.

The organization that has, perhaps, actually saved more land than any other nongovernmental organization is The Nature Conservancy, a low-profile group that preserves unique ecosystems through purchase, gifts, or easements. Sydney Macy, director of the Colorado Nature Conservancy, calls the prairie "a vibrant place" and regrets that "most people see only badly overgrazed prairie or just bits and pieces such as the triangular patches that are not watered by the circular irrigation systems."

It has been estimated that less than 1 percent of the original prairie ecosystem remains, and it's at least in part because of The Nature Conservancy that some of the best has been protected. So far, however, the emphasis has been on saving tallgrass and mixed-grass prairie rather than shortgrass prairie.

Bits and pieces of prairie—about 117,000 hectares (289,000 acres)—have been preserved in national parks or monuments in the Great Plains, according to James Stubbendieck, Range Ecology Professor at the University of Nebraska. Stubbendieck recently compiled *An Identification of Prairie in National Park Units in the Great Plains*, a mammoth undertaking that lists thirty-two national parks and monuments that contain prairie. However, only 810 hectares (2000 acres) are devoted to shortgrass.

Few people are even aware of a proposal for a Great Plains National Park that would include both mixed and short grasses. Durward Allen—writer, researcher, teacher, and conservationist—proposed such a park in 1976 to fill "the hole in the system." Addressing the First Conference on Scientific Research in the National Parks, he said, "We have no major park that truly represents the Great Plains, and the grasslands in general have been neglected."

Even in 1976 the idea was not new. Allen credits Victor Shelford with suggesting the idea to the Park Service as early as 1930 and Victor Cahalane with drawing up detailed plans in 1940. Almost a century before that, Chief Seattle, head of the Suquamish tribe, spoke in anguish about the "stranger who comes in the night and takes from the land whatever he needs." Although he wasn't referring to the shortgrass prairie, his words seem sadly fitting. Forced to sell his tribe's lands, he pled, "You must keep it apart and sacred as a place where even the white man can go to taste the wind that is sweetened by the meadow's flowers."

For a Great Plains Park to work as a viable eco-system, it must be large. "Size is part of the ecology of the grassland community," says Allen. "A million-acre park (nearly half the size of Yellowstone) will be much more than the sum of its parts." He also cautions, "Grassland is not just grass, and its true beauty and productivity cannot be appreciated unless it is complete with its natural complement of forbs and animal life."

Allen still hopes for such a park and believes it could be located in the tri-state area where South Dakota, Nebraska, and Wyoming meet. He does not like to pinpoint an exact location for fear of arous-

Mountain plover: Pawnee National Grassland, Colorado

Left—
Sandhill cranes on the
South Platte River:
Kearney, Nebraska

ing local opposition. He writes: "A fenced park of the type I have recommended would preserve the entire grassland ecosystem with a minimum of human interference. That would include the wolf, which in turn would mean that the bison and other ungulates would be subject to the culling that is natural for such species. As the situation stands now, south of Canada, the bison is being converted into a domestic animal."

William Mott, director of the National Park Service, has been pushing for many years for a Tallgrass Prairie National Preserve and believes that legislation will be passed soon establishing such a preserve in Oklahoma. However, he says, "No legislation is being proposed or even discussed on the idea of a Shortgrass Prairie Park or a Great Plains Park. That's not to say it shouldn't be, but someone at the grassroots level has to stimulate something of that sort.

"We need representative examples of the various ecosystems in the national parks," he says. "I think shortgrass ought to be part of the National Park System for future generations to enjoy." Mott admits that in the past "I had the vision the prairies were relatively flat and uninteresting." Now that he knows them better, he finds them interesting, historically valuable, and beautiful. "When the wind blows," he says, "it gives you almost the sense of an ocean."

Below—
Great blue heron and ducks:
Sawhill Ponds, Colorado

CHAPTER SIX

The vastness. . . . You can look
east. You can look south. You can
look back up the canyons. It's an
immense thing—this, this space.
—Earl Johnson, Rancher

Revery

Part of the fun of writing this book was talking to so many different people who were concerned about the prairie. They were a diverse lot and did not always agree on how best to care for the prairie or even what constitutes a short-grass prairie. But they all loved it. When asked "What do you like best about the prairie?" most of them gave such apt replies that we decided to end our book with those answers.

Left—
Sunset:
Monument Rocks, Kansas
Right—
Blackbird, cattails:
Sawhill Ponds, Colorado

"I guess it's the scale of them; they're sort of subtle, and the appreciation of them is subtle. They look the same from a distance, and to really appreciate them you have to look up close to see all the differences"– Sue Galatowitsch, Ecologist, Colorado Natural Areas Program.

"The diversity. . . . If you're in a spruce-fir forest, there's practically nothing, but if you're in the grasslands, there are orders of magnitude more species. . . . You have to get down on your hands and knees to realize how scenic it is." — Betsy Webb, Zoologist, Denver Museum of Natural History.

"It seems to be a constant contradiction of itself. It is delicate, yet resilient; it appears to be simple, but closer inspection indicates that it is extremely complex; it may appear monotonous, but it is diverse and ever-changing throughout the seasons."—James Stubbendieck, Professor, University of Nebraska.

"The feeling of open space and freedom . . . and the tremendous variety that exists here when a person is attuned to what's going on with the plants and animals."—Dale Lasater, rancher.

"The space and the peacefulness of it. . . . It seemingly rolls without end even in this modern time." — Warren Whitman, Professor of Botany, North Dakota State University.

"I can see forever. . . . It is an environment where nothing comes between me, the sky, the horizons, and my dreams."—Ed Butterfield, Grassland Institute.

"The remoteness of it, the essential pristineness of it. . . . I'm seeing the world without man's enormous hand on it, and I feel good about this. It brings it home to me what my responsibilities as a human are. Most of society never has that opportunity, that necessity. . . . we have lost this contact with earth." — Willard Louden, rancher.

"The way it makes me feel when I'm there (and when I'm thinking about it!). To me, it somehow exemplifies freedom — of space, of thoughts, of movement, and of time." — Brian Sindelar, Professor of Range Sciences, Montana State University.

Selected Places To See Shortgrass Prairie

Most of the sites in Colorado, New Mexico, Oklahoma, and Texas are pure shortgrass prairie. The others contain a mixture of mid, short, and tall grasses. Many of them are also important historically.

COLORADO

The Plains Conservation Center
21901 E. Hampden Ave., Aurora, CO 80013
Described in text.

Bent's Old Fort National Historic Site
35110 Highway 194 East, La Junta, CO 81050
This reconstructed fort was once the most important trading post between Independence, Missouri, and Santa Fe, New Mexico.

Central Plains Experimental Range
c/o Bill Lauenroth, Dept. of Range Science
Fort Collins, CO 80523
Much of the research literature on the shortgrass prairie comes from this station, which is administered by the Agricultural Research Service.

Comanche National Grassland
San Isabel N.F., Pueblo, CO 81008
Located near La Junta, Colorado. Picture and Carrizo canyons are outstanding topographic features. Lesser prairie chickens and long-billed curlews can sometimes be seen.

Denver Botanic Gardens
909 York St., Denver, CO 80206
Restoration described in text.

Denver Museum of Natural History
City Park, Denver, CO 80205
Fossils from the Great Plains, including dinosaurs, mammoths, camels, horses, rhinoceroses, and prehistoric fish are displayed here as well as realistic dioramas showing the ecology of the plains, past and present.

Pawnee National Grassland
2017 9th St., Greeley, CO 80631
Located in northeastern Colorado near Ault and Briggsdale. The Pawnee Buttes, made famous by James Michener in *Centennial*, dominate this grassland, which is also a mecca for birdwatchers.

KANSAS

Cimarron National Grassland
737 Villy Maca St., Elkhart, KS 67950
Riparian areas along the Cimarron River, "Point of Rocks" (a landmark on the Cimarron Cutoff of the Santa Fe Trail), and lesser prairie chicken leks are noteworthy.

Fort Larned National Historic Site
Route 3, Larned, KS 67550
Ruts of the Santa Fe Trail are still visible in places. Several different types of prairie and a shortgrass prairie restoration can be seen here.

Lake Scott State Park
Route 1, Scott City, KS 67871
An elk herd, a labeled nature trail, swimming, canoeing, and an Indian pueblo ruin are only a few of the

joys of one of our favorite state parks. The nearby Monument Rocks, eroded monoliths from the Cretaceous Sea, should also be seen.

NEBRASKA

Agate Fossil Beds National Monument
P.O. Box 427, Gering, NE 69341
Sedimentary rocks contain animal fossils from twenty million years ago, and nearby formations contain agates. A good botanical trail names the prairie plants.

Chimney Rock National Historic Site
c/o Scotts Bluff National Monument (see below)
Pioneers along the Oregon Trail looked for Chimney Rock as an important landmark on their journey and carved their names in its clay. Here you can see badlands as well as prairie.

Oglala National Grassland
P.O. Box 13A9, Chadron, NE 69337
Borders Wyoming and South Dakota. Toadstool Park with its strangely shaped rocks is the best-known feature of this grassland, which is also famous for the Hudson-Meng Buffalo Kill Site.

Scotts Bluff National Monument
P.O. Box 427, Gering, NE 69341
The 800-foot promontory looming above the North Platte Valley was also a landmark for early pioneers on the Oregon Trail. Later, the Pony Express crossed through here.

NEW MEXICO

Capulin Mountain National Monument
Capulin, NM 88414
The cone of a recently extinct volcano rises 1000 feet above the surrounding shortgrass prairie and forest. A trail leads into the crater.

Fort Union National Monument
Watrous, NM 87753
Remnants of the Santa Fe Trail and the remains of three forts built to defend New Mexico Territory during the last half of the nineteenth century can be explored.

Kiowa National Grassland
16 North 2nd St., Clayton, NM 88415
The 500-foot deep Canadian River Canyon and remnants of the Santa Fe Trail Cimarron Cutoff are highlights of this grassland, which in 1981 became the first unit of the Forest Service to try Allan Savory's approach to grazing with great success.

NORTH DAKOTA

Fort Union Trading Post National Historic Site
Buford Route, Williston, ND 58801
Located at the confluence of the Yellowstone and Missouri rivers and lying partly in Montana, this fort has been important in American history since the Lewis and Clark expeditions.

Theodore Roosevelt National Park
Medora, ND 58645
Badlands, bison, and rolling prairie along the Little Missouri River make this a favorite national park for many people who want to avoid the crowds at more famous parks. It also includes part of Theodore Roosevelt's Elkhorn Ranch.

OKLAHOMA

Black Kettle National Grassland
P.O. Box 266, Cheyenne, OK 73628
Recreational lakes as well as prairie can be enjoyed in this grassland, which includes units in both Oklahoma and Texas.

Black Mesa State Park
Kenton, OK 73946
Prehistoric Indians left pictographs; Coronado (possibly) left an inscription on a canyon wall; the Santa Fe Trail crossed it; and Kit Carson established a fort here at the highest point in Oklahoma. Ears of corn and pumpkin vines suggest this may have been one of the earliest agricultural areas in the U.S.

SOUTH DAKOTA

Badlands National Park
P.O. Box 6, Interior, SD 57750
Bizarre geological formations, animal fossils, interesting wildlife, and good hiking trails are the attractions here.

Buffalo Gap National Grassland
Black Hills N. F., Custer, SD 57730
Located near Hot Springs, Wall, and Rapid City, this site includes badlands, woodland draws, and Fairburn agates.

Custer State Park
Five miles east of Custer on U.S. 16A
Mostly midgrass prairie, this park in the Black Hills sustains one of the world's largest remaining bison herds.

Mammoth Site
One and one-half miles southwest of Hot Springs on U.S. 18 bypass
The largest concentration of mammoth bones in the western hemisphere has been excavated from this ancient sinkhole. Partially excavated mammoths and other prehistoric animal skeletons can be seen inside the visitor center that has been built to protect the site. Also visit the Claude A. Barr prairie/plains garden.

Wind Cave National Park
Hot Springs, SD 57747
The limestone caverns with guided tours (including historic tours by candlelight) usually outshine the shimmering Black Hills prairie, which is itself well worth an extra day to enjoy.

TEXAS

Alibates Flint Quarries National Monument
c/o Lake Meredith Recreation Area
P.O. Box 1438, Fritch, TX 79036
Prehistoric Indians of the High Plains used this flint for tools and weapons. Has been heavily grazed in the past but is now covered mainly by blue grama.

Buffalo Lake National Wildlife Refuge
P.O. Box 228, Umbarger, TX 79091
The High Plains Natural Area within the Buffalo NWR is an undisturbed climax shortgrass prairie— something that is almost impossible to find. The shallow lakes or "playas" here and at Muleshoe NWR attract enormous populations of waterfowl.

Muleshoe National Wildlife Refuge
P.O. Box 549, Muleshoe, TX 79347
Wintering sandhill cranes and waterfowl are the chief attractions.

Rita Blanca National Grassland
P.O. Box 38, Texline, TX 79087
Long-billed curlews breed in this grassland located partly in Texas and partly in Oklahoma.

WYOMING

Fort Laramie National Historic Site
Fort Laramie, WY 82212
During the nineteenth century this was the site of a fur trading and military post, much of which has been restored. A museum is also available.

Guernsey State Park
Three miles west of Guernsey off.U.S. 26
Here you can enjoy hiking, fishing, water sports, and a museum. Don't miss two nearby historic sites: Oregon Trail Ruts, where the covered wagons wore grooves five to six feet deep, and Register Cliff, where thousands of westering pioneers carved their names.

Thunder Basin National Grassland
Medicine Bow N. F., Laramie, WY 82070
Located in the northeastern corner of the state near Douglas and Gillette. Hunting is the chief recreation in this grassland, which includes hundreds of oil and gas wells and three operating coal strip mines. Reclamation is being undertaken.

Animals of the Shortgrass Prairie

BIRDS

Species listed are those found throughout the area covered in this book. Rare or geographically isolated species have been omitted. Because the shortgrass prairie stretches from Canada to southern Texas, the seasonal designations are only rough indications of most likely occurrences. For instance, a species listed as migrant might also be a summer or winter resident in some regions.

R – Year-round resident   W – Winter resident
M – Migrant   S – Summer resident

Grebes
Clark's grebe   R
Western grebe   R
Pied-billed grebe   S, M

Pelicans, Cormorants, and Herons
American white pelican   S
Double-crested cormorant   S
Great blue heron   R
Black-crowned night heron   S
American bittern   S

Waterfowl
Canada goose   R
Snow goose   M
Mallard   R
Gadwall   R
Pintail   R
Green-winged teal   R
Blue-winged teal   S, M
Cinnamon teal   S, M
American wigeon   W, M
Northern shoveler   R
Redhead   R
Canvasback   W, M
Lesser scaup   R
Common goldeneye   W, M
Bufflehead   W, M
Ruddy duck   S, M
Hooded merganser   W, M
Common merganser   R
Red-breasted merganser   M

Vultures, Eagles, Hawks, and Falcons
Turkey vulture   M
Red-tailed hawk   R
Swainson's hawk   S
Rough-legged hawk   W
Ferruginous hawk   R
Golden eagle   R
Bald eagle   W
Northern harrier   R
Prairie falcon   R
American kestrel   R

Game birds
Ring-necked pheasant   R
Northern bobwhite   R

Rails and coots
Virginia rail   S
Sora   S
American coot   R

Shorebirds
   Mountain plover   S
   Killdeer   R
   Common snipe   R
   Long-billed curlew   S
   Spotted sandpiper   S
   Greater yellowlegs   M
   Lesser yellowlegs   M
   Baird's sandpiper   M
   Least sandpiper   M
   Long-billed dowitcher   M
   Semipalmated sandpiper   M
   Western sandpiper   M
   American avocet   S
   Wilson's phalarope   S

Gulls and Terns
   Herring gull   W
   California gull   S
   Ring-billed gull   R
   Franklin's gull   S, M
   Forster's tern   S
   Black tern   S

Doves, Owls, and Nightjars
   Rock dove   R
   Mourning dove   S
   Eastern screech owl   R
   Great-horned owl   R
   Long-eared owl   R
   Short-eared owl   R
   Burrowing owl   S
   Poor-will   S
   Common nighthawk   S

Kingfisher
   Belted kingfisher   R

Woodpeckers
   Northern flicker   R
   Red-headed woodpecker   R
   Downy woodpecker   R

Flycatchers, Larks, and Swallows
   Eastern kingbird   S
   Western kingbird   S
   Say's phoebe   S
   Western wood pewee   S
   Horned lark   R
   Barn swallow   S
   Cliff swallow   S
   Bank swallow   S

Jays, Crows, Chickadees, and Creepers
   Blue jay   R
   Black-billed magpie   R
   Common raven   R
   American crow   R
   Black-capped chickadee   R
   Brown creeper   R

Wrens
   House wren   S
   Long-billed marsh wren   R
   Canyon wren   R
   Rock wren   S

Thrushes, Thrashers, and Shrikes
   Mockingbird   S
   Brown thrasher   S
   American robin   R

Swainson's thrush   S
Northern shrike   W
Loggerhead shrike   S
Mountain bluebird   M

Starlings
Starling   R

Warblers
Yellow warbler   S
Common yellowthroat   S

Grosbeaks and Buntings
Blue grosbeak   S
Indigo bunting   S
Lazuli bunting   S

Sparrows and Finches
House finch   R
American goldfinch   R
Lark bunting   S
Savannah sparrow   S
Grasshopper sparrow   S
Vesper sparrow   S
Lark sparrow   S
Tree sparrow   W
Chipping sparrow   S
Clay-colored sparrow   M
Brewer's sparrow   S
McCown's longspur   S
Lapland longspur   W
Chestnut-collared longspur   S
House sparrow   R

Meadowlarks, Blackbirds, and Orioles
Western meadowlark   R
Yellow-headed blackbird   S
Red-winged blackbird   R
Brewer's blackbird   S
Northern oriole   S
Orchard oriole   S
Common grackle   S
Brown-headed cowbird   S

MAMMALS
(Does not include extirpated species)

Insectivores
Masked shrew
Least shrew

Bats
Little brown bat
Long-legged myotis
Small-footed myotis
Silver-haired bat
Big brown bat
Hoary bat

Rabbits
Eastern cottontail
Desert cottontail
White-tailed jackrabbit
Black-tailed jackrabbit

Rodents
Thirteen-lined ground squirrel
Spotted ground squirrel
Black-tailed prairie dog
Fox squirrel
Plains pocket gopher
Olive-backed pocket mouse
Plains pocket mouse
Hispid pocket mouse
Ord's kangaroo rat
Beaver
Plains harvest mouse

Western harvest mouse
Deer mouse
Northern grasshopper mouse
Meadow vole
Prairie vole
Muskrat
Porcupine

Carnivores
Coyote
Red fox
Swift fox
Raccoon
Long-tailed weasel
Black-footed ferret
Badger
Striped skunk

Ungulates
Wapiti, or elk
Mule deer
White-tailed deer
Pronghorn
Bison

Common Plants of the Shortgrass Prairie Region

This list includes some plants found in lowland riparian ecosystems (along streams) and scarp woodlands (atop bluffs) as well as those found in the shortgrass prairie ecosystem itself. In cases where individual species of a particular genus are difficult to identify, or where a genus is represented by many species but only a few species are common, the genus name is listed followed by the abbreviation "spp." (multiple species). Since plant taxonomy is always in a state of flux, we have taken scientific names from a single source, *Flora of the Great Plains*, compiled and edited by R. I. McGregor and T. M. Barkley. Common names vary from region to region; in cases where obvious ambiguities exist, we have listed a second common name in parenthesis.

TREES

Ash, green *Fraxinus pennsylvanica*
Box-elder *Acer negundo*
Cottonwood, plains *Populus deltoides*
Elm *Ulmus* spp.
  American *U. americana*
  Siberian *U. pumila*
Hackberry *Celtis occidentalis, C. reticulata*
Juniper (Red cedar) *Juniperus scopulorum*
Pine, limber *Pinus flexilis*
Pine, ponderosa *Pinus ponderosa*
Russian-olive *Elaeagnus angustifolia*
Willows *Salix* spp.
  coyote (sandbar) *S. exigua*
  peachleaf *S. amygdaloides*

SHRUBS

Chokecherry *Prunus virginiana*
Honey mesquite *Prosopis glandulosa*
Mountain mahogany *Cercocarpus montanus*
Plum, wild *Prunus americana*
Rabbitbrush *Chrysothamnus nauseosus*
Roses *Rosa* spp.
  prairie wild *R. arkansana*
  western wild *R. woodsii*
Sagebrushes *Artemisia* spp.
  sand *A. filifolia*
  western *A. campestris*
  white *A. ludoviciana*
Saltbrushes *Atriplex* spp.
  shadscale (four-winged) *A. canescens*
  silverscale *A. argentea*
Serviceberry *Amelanchier alnifolia*
Snowberry *Symphoricarpos occidentalis*
Sumac, aromatic (Skunkbrush) *Rhus* spp.
Winterfat *Ceratoides lanata*

GRASSES

Barley, foxtail *Hordeum jubatum*
Bluestems *Andropogon* spp.
  big *A. gerardi*
  little *A. scoparius*
Bromes *Bromus* spp.
  cheatgrass *B. tectorum*
  smooth *B. inermis*
Buffalo grass *Buchloë dactyloides*
Dropseed, sand *Sporobolus cryptandrus*

Gramas *Bouteloua* spp.
  blue *B. gracilis*
  side-oats *B. curtipendula*
June grass *Koeleria pyramidata*
Muhlies *Muhlenbergia* spp.
  alkali *M. asperifolia*
  marsh *M. racemosa*
Needle grasses *Stipa* spp.
  green *S. viridula*
  needle-and-thread *S. comata*
Ricegrass, Indian *Oryzopsis hymenoides*
Squirreltail *Sitanion hystrix*
Switchgrass *Panicum virgatum*
Three-awn, red *Aristida purpurea*
Wheatgrass, western *Agropyron smithii*

GRASS-LIKE PLANTS

Bulrushes *Scirpus* spp.
  chair-maker's rush *S. americanus*
  dark green *S. atrovirens*
  hard-stem *S. acutus*
  prairie *S. maritimus*
  soft-stem *S. validus*
Bur-reed, giant *Sparganium eurycarpum*
Cattails *Typha* spp.
  narrow-leaved *T. angustifolia*
  common *T. latifolia*
Duckweed *Lemna minor*
Horsetail, smooth *Equisetum laevigatum*
Pondweeds *Potamogeton* spp.
Rushes *Juncus* spp.
  Baltic *J. balticus*
  Dudley's *J. dudleyi*

inland *J. interior*
Torrey's *J. torreyi*
Sedges *Carex* spp.

FORBS

Asparagus *Asparagus officinalis*
Asters *Aster* spp.
  white *A. ericoides*
  white prairie *A. falcatus*
  panicled *A. hesperius*
Beeplant, Rocky Mountain *Cleome serrulata*
Bindweeds *Convolvulus* spp.
  field *C. arvensis*
  hedge *C. sepium*
Black-eyed Susan *Rudbeckia hirta*
Blazingstar (Gayfeather) *Liatris punctata*
Buttercups *Ranunculus* spp.
  cursed crowfoot *R. sceleratus*
  Macoun's *R. macounii*
  shore *R. cymbalaria*
  white water crowfoot *R. longirostris*
Cactus, pincushion *Corypantha vivipara*
Cactus, prickly pears *Opuntia* spp.
Camas, death *Zigadenus venenosus*
Chickory, common *Cichorium intybus*
Clovers *Trifolium* spp.
  red *T. pratense*
  white *T. repens*
Coneflower, prairie *Ratibida columnifera*
  purple *Echinacea angustifolia*
Coreopsis, plains *Coreopsis tinctoria*
Dandelion, common *Taraxacum officinale*

Docks *Rumex* spp.
Evening-primroses *Oenothera* spp.
  common *O. strigosa*
  prairie *O. albicaulis*
  white stemless *O. caespitosa*
  yellow stemless *O. brachycarpa*
Evening-stars *Mentzelia* spp.
  giant *M. decapetala*
  many-flowered *M. multiflora*
  plains *M. nuda*
Flax, blue *Linum lewisii*
  stiffstem *L. rigidum*
Fleabanes *Erigeron* spp.
Four-o'clock, Narrowleaf *Mirabilis linearis*
  wild *M. nyctaginea*
Gaura, scarlet *Gaura coccinea*
  velvety *G. parviflora*
Globemallow, scarlet *Sphaeralcea coccinea*
Goldenrods *Solidago* spp.
Gromwell, false *Onosmodium molle*
Hemp, Indian (Dogbane) *Apocynum* spp.
Hymenoxys, stemless *Hymenoxys acaulis*
Gourd, wild (Buffalo) *Cucurbita foetidissima*
Gumweed *Grindelia squarrosa*
Lupine, low (small) *Lupinus pusillus*
  silvery (Nebraska) *L. argenteus (plattensis)*
Licorice, wild *Glycyrrhiza lepidota*
Larkspur, prairie *Delphinium virescens*
Locoweed, purple *Oxytropis lambertii*
  white *O. sericea*
Lettuce, blue *Lactuca oblongifolia*
  prickly *L. serriola*

Milkvetches *Astragalus* spp.
  ceramic *A. ceramicus*
  ground plum *A. crassicarpus, A. plattensis*
  Missouri *A. missouriensis*
  narrow-leaved poisonvetch *A. pectinatus*
  slender *A. gracilis*
  woolly loco *A. mollissimus*
Milkweeds *Asclepias* spp.
  dwarf *A. pumila*
  green *A. veridiflora*
  showy *A. speciosa*
  swamp *A. incarnata*
Morning-glory, bush *Ipomoea leptophylla*
Mullein, great *Verbascum thapsus*
Mustards *Brassica* spp.
Onion, wild *Allium* spp.
Paintbrush, plains *Castilleja sessiliflora*
Penstemons *Penstemon* spp.
  narrow beardtongue *P. angustifolius*
  white beardtongue *P. albidus*
Pepper-grasses *Lepidium* spp.
Pigweeds *Amaranthus* spp.
  common (tumbleweed) *A. albus*
  rough *A. retroflexus*
Plantains *Plantago* spp.
  buckhorn *P. patagonica*
  common *P. major*
Phlox *Phlox* spp.
  Hood's *P. hoodii*
  moss *P. andicola*
Poppy, prickly *Argemone polyanthemos*
Poppy-mallow, purple *Callirhoë involucrata*

Prairie clovers *Petalostemon* spp.
  purple *P. purpureum*
  western *P. occidentale*
  white *P. candidum*
Puccoon, narrow-leaved *Lithospermum incisum*
Purslane, common *Portulaca oleracea*
Pussytoes *Antennaria* spp.
Ragweed, western *Ambrosia psilostachya*
Ragwort *Senecio* spp.
Sage, pasture *Artemisia frigida*
Sand-lily *Leucocrinum montanum*
Salsify *Tragopogon* spp.
Sand-verbena *Abronia fragrans*
Snakeweed *Gutierrezia sarothrae*
Snow-on-the-mountain *Euphorbia marginata*
Spiderwort *Tradescantia occidentalis*
Sulphur-flowers *Eriogonum* spp.
Sunflowers *Helianthus* spp.
  common *H. annuus*
  prairie *H. petiolaris*
Thistle, Canada *Cirsium arvense*
  Russian *Salsola iberica*
Townsendias *Townsendia* spp.
  Easter daisy *T. exscapa*
  large-flowered *T. grandiflora*
Verbenas (Vervains) *Verbena* spp.
  blue *V. hastata*
  bracted *V. bractiata*
  woolly *V. stricta*
Wallflower, western *Erysimum asperum*
Yellow cress *Rorippa* spp.
Yucca *Yucca glauca*

BOOKS

Allen, Durward Leon. *The Life of Prairies and Plains*. New York: McGraw Hill, 1967.

Allen, Thomas B. et al. *Field Guide to the Birds of North America*. Washington, D.C.: National Geographic Society, 1983.

Armstrong, David M. *Distribution of Mammals in Colorado*. Monograph of the Museum of Natural History, University of Kansas, No. 3. Lawrence: Museum of Natural History, University of Kansas, 1972.

Athearn, Robert G. *High Country Empire: The High Plains and Rockies*. Lincoln: Univ. of Nebraska Press, 1960.

Audubon Society Master Guide to Birding. New York: Alfred A. Knopf, 1983.

Bakker, Robert T. *The Dinosaur Heresies*. New York: William Morrow, 1986.

Barsness, Larry. *Heads, Hides and Horns*. Fort Worth: Texas Christian Univ. Press, 1985.

Bent, George. *Life of George Bent, Written From His Letters* by George E. Hyde. Norman: Univ. of Oklahoma Press, 1968.

Bingham, Sam, and Eddie Lee, Rex Lee Jim, and the Rock Point Range Management Project. *Living From Livestock*. Chinle, AZ: Rock Point Community School, 1984.

Black Elk. *Black Elk Speaks, Being the Life Story of a Holy Man of the Oglala Sioux* as told through John G. Neihardt. New York: Pocket Books, a division of Simon & Schuster, 1972.

Borland, Hal. *High, Wide and Lonesome*. Philadelphia: J. B. Lippincott, 1956.

Brown, Lauren. *Grasslands*. The Audubon Society Nature Guides. New York: Alfred A. Knopf, 1985.

Buechel, Eugene. *Dictionary of the Teton-Dakota Sioux Language*. Pine Ridge, S.D.: Red Cloud Indian School, Holy Rosary Mission, 1970.

Burland, Cottie Arthur. *North American Indian Mythology*. New York: Peter Bedrick Books, 1985.

Burton, Richard Francis. *The City of Saints*. New York: Alfred A. Knopf, 1963.

Cassells, E. Steve. *The Archaeology of Colorado*. Boulder: Johnson Books, 1983.

Cather, Willa. *My Antonia*. Boston: Houghton Mifflin, 1954.

Catlin, George. *Letters and Notes on the North American Indians*, edited and with an introduction by Michael MacDonald Mooney. New York: Clarkson N. Potter, 1975.

Chronic, Halka. *Roadside Geology of Colorado*. Missoula: Mountain Press, 1980.

Chronic, Halka. *Pages of Stone: Geology of Western National Parks and Monuments*. Vol. 1. Seattle: The Mountaineers, 1984.

Clemens, Samuel L. *Roughing It*. New York: Harper, 1899.

Colbert, Edwin Harris. *Dinosaurs, An Illustrated History*. Maplewood, NJ: Hammond, 1983.

Collins, Lawrence T., ed. *Natural Kansas*. Lawrence: Univ. Press of Kansas, 1985.

Costello, David F. *The Prairie World*. New York: Thomas Y. Crowell, 1969.

Dary, David A. *The Buffalo Book*. New York: Avon Books, 1974.

Dickinson, Emily. *Selected Poems*. New York: Random House, 1924.

Dort, Wakefield, Jr. and J. Knox Jones, Jr., editors. *Pleistocene and Recent Environments of the Central Great Plains*. Lawrence: Univ. Press of Kansas, 1970.

Eide, Ingvard Henry, Comp. *American Odyssey: The Journey of Lewis and Clark*. Chicago: Rand McNally, 1969.

Ewan, Joseph Andorfer. *Rocky Mountain Naturalists*. Denver: Univ. of Denver Press, 1956.

Frémont, John Charles. *Narratives of Exploration and Adventure*, Edited by Allan Nevins. New York: Longmans, Green, 1956.

Goetzmann, William H. *Exploration and Empire: The Explorer and the Scientist in the Winning of the American West.* New York: Alfred A. Knopf, 1966.

Grassland and Tundra, by the editors of Time-Life Books. Alexandria, VA: Time-Life Books, 1984.

Gregg, Josiah. *Commerce of the Prairies*, edited by Max L. Moorhead. Norman: Oklahoma Univ. Press, 1954.

Haines, Francis. *The Plains Indians*. New York: Thomas Crowell, 1976.

Haley, James Evetts. *Charles Goodnight, Cowman and Plainsman.* Norman: Oklahoma Univ. Press, 1936.

Hughes, Johnson Donald. *American Indians in Colorado.* Boulder: Pruett, 1977.

Ise, John. *Sod and Stubble*. Lincoln: Univ. of Nebraska Press, 1968, c.1936.

Jackson, Wes. *New Roots for American Agriculture*. San Francisco: Friends of the Earth, 1980.

James, Edwin. *Account of an Expedition from Pittsburgh to the Rocky Mountains.* Philadelphia: H. C. Carey & I. Lea, 1823.

Jones, Charles Jesse. *Buffalo Jones' Forty Years of Adventure*, compiled by Henry Inman. Topeka: Crane, 1899.

Kozlowski, T. T. and C. E. Ahlgren, editors. *Fire and Ecosystems.* New York: Academic Press, 1974.

Kurten, Bjorn and Elaine Anderson. *Pleistocene Mammals of North America*. New York: Columbia Univ. Press, 1980.

Lewis, Meriwether. *History of the Expedition Under the Command of Captains Lewis and Clark*, prepared for the press by Paul Allen. Chicago: A. C. McClurg, 1902.

Low, Ann Marie. *Dust Bowl Diary*. Lincoln: University of Nebraska Press, 1984.

Lowie, Robert Harry. *Indians of the Plains*. New York: McGraw Hill, 1954.

McGregor, R. L. and T. M. Barkley, editors. *Atlas of the Flora of the Great Plains*. Ames: Iowa State University Press, 1977.

McGregor, R. L. and T. M. Barkley. *Flora of the Great Plains*. Ames: Iowa State University Press, 1986.

McPhee, John. *Rising from the Plains*. New York: Farrar, Strauss, Giroux, 1986.

Madson, John. *Where the Sky Began*. Boston: Houghton Mifflin, 1982.

McDonald, Jerry N. *North American Bison*. Berkeley: Univ. of California Press, 1981.

McHugh, Tom. *The Time of the Bison*. New York: Alfred A. Knopf, 1972.

Michener, James A. *Centennial*. New York: Random House, 1974.

Muilenburg, Grace. *Land of the Post Rock*. Lawrence: Univ. Press of Kansas, 1975.

Mutel, Cornelia and John Emerick. *From Grassland to Glacier, the Natural History of Colorado*. Boulder: Johnson, 1984.

O'Brien, Lynne Woods. *Plains Indian Autobiographies*. Boise State College Western Writers Series #10. Boise: Boise State College, 1973.

Parkman, Francis. *The Oregon Trail*. Garden City: Doubleday, 1946.

Pike, Zebulon Montgomery. *The Expeditions of Zebulon Montgomery Pike*, edited by Elliott Coues. Vol. 2. New York: Harper, 1895.

Roe, Frank Gilbert. *The North American Buffalo: A Critical Study of the Species in Its Wild State*. Toronto: Univ. of Toronto Press, 1951.

Rolvaag, Ole Edvart. *Giants in the Earth*. New York: Harper, 1927.

Roosevelt, Theodore. *The Wilderness Hunter*. New York: Current Literature Publishing, 1907.

Rorabacher, J. Albert. *The American Buffalo in Transition; A Historical and Economic Survey*. St. Cloud, MN: North Star Press, 1970.

Sandoz, Mari. *Old Jules*. Boston: Little Brown, 1935.

Sandoz, Mari. *Love Song to the Plains*. New York: Harper, 1961.

Sanford, Mollie Dorsey. *Mollie*. Lincoln: Univ. of Nebraska Press, 1959.

Snyder, Gerald S. *In the Footsteps of Lewis and Clark*. Washington, D.C.: National Geographic Society, 1970.

Standing Bear, Luther. *Land of the Spotted Eagle*. Lincoln: Univ. of Nebraska Press, 1978.

Stoke, Will E. *Episodes of Early Days in Central and Western Kansas*. Great Bend, KS: Will E. Stoke, 1926.

Stratton, Joanna L. *Pioneer Women: Voices from the Kansas Frontier*. New York: Simon & Schuster, 1981.

Suttcliffe, Anthony John. *On the Track of Ice Age Mammals*. Cambridge: Harvard University Press, 1985.

Svobida, Lawrence. *Farming the Dust Bowl*. Lawrence: Univ. Press of Kansas, 1986.

Two Leggings. *Two Leggings: The Making of a Crow Warrior*, edited by Peter Nabokov. New York: Thomas Y. Crowell, 1967.

Van Wormer, Joe. *The World of the Pronghorn*. Philadelphia: J. B. Lippincott, 1969.

Vanderwerth, W. C., Comp. *Indian Oratory*. Norman, OK.: Univ. of Oklahoma Press, 1971.

Weaver, John Ernest. *North American Prairies*. Lincoln: Johnsen, 1954.

Weaver, John Ernest. *Grasslands of the Great Plains*. Lincoln: Johnsen, 1956.

Webb, Walter Prescott. *The Great Plains*. New York: Grosset & Dunlap, 1931.

Weber, William A. *Rocky Mountain Flora*. Boulder, CO: Colorado Associated University Press, 1976.

Weimer, Robert J. and John D. Haun. *Guide to the Geology of Colorado*. Denver: Geological Society of America, 1960.

Welsch, Roger. *Shingling the Fog and Other Plains Lies*. Chicago: Sage Books, 1972.

Whitaker, John O. *The Audubon Society Field Guide to North American Mammals*. New York: Alfred Knopf, 1984.

Williams, Oscar Waldo. *Pioneer Surveyor, Frontier Lawyer; The Personal Narrative of O. W. Williams, 1877–1902*, edited by S. D. Myres. El Paso: Western College Press, 1966.

Winship, George Parker, editor. *The Coronado Expedition, 1540–1542*. Chicago: Rio Grande Press, 1964.

Worster, Donald. *Dust Bowl; The Southern Plains in the 1930s*. New York: Oxford University Press, 1979.

JOURNAL AND NEWSPAPER ARTICLES

Allen, Durward. "The Hole in the System: A Great Plains National Park." In *First Conference on Scientific Research in the National Parks*, edited by Robert M. Linn, 1 (1976): 5–8.

Allen, Durward. "A Proposal: Great Plains National Park." *National Parks & Conservation Magazine* 51 (August 1977): 4–9.

Berger, John J. "The Prairie Makers." *Sierra* 70 (November/December 1985): 66–70.

Bingham, Sam. "Allan Savory: Creator of a Socratic Approach To Land Management." *High Country News* 19 (April 27, 1987): 11+.

Blume, Ed. "The American Prairies: a State of Mind." *Horticulture* 57 (August 1979): 52+.

Bonham, Charles D. and Alton Lerwick. "Vegetation Changes Induced by Prairie Dogs on Shortgrass Range." *Journal of Range Management* 29 (May 1976): 221–225.

Bryson, Reid A. "Chinook Climates and Plains Peoples." *Great Plains Quarterly* 1 (Winter 1981): 5–15.

Cable, Dwight R. "Fire Effects on Semidesert Grasses and Shrubs." *Journal of Range Management* 20 (May 1967): 170–176.

Carrels, Peter. "There Are No Boring Landscapes." *High Country News* 18 (October 27, 1986): 14–15.

Chiszar, David, David Dickman, and Joel Colton. "Sensitivity to Thermal Stimulation in Prairie Rattlesnakes." *Behavioral and Neural Biology* 45 (January 1986): 143–149.

Collins, Scott L. and Susan C. Barber. "Effects of Disturbance on Diversity in Mixed-grass Prairie." *Vegetatio* 64 (January 1986): 87–94.

Coss, Richard G. and Donald H. Owings. "Snake-directed Behavior by Snake Naive and Experienced California Ground Squirrels in a Simulated Burrow." *Zeitshrift Fur Tierpsychology* 48 (December 1978): 421–435.

Costello, David F. "Natural Vegetation of Abandoned Plowed Land in the Mixed Prairie Association of Northeastern Colorado." *Ecology* 25 (July 1944): 312–326.

Cushman, Ruth Carol. "Where the Avocet and the Antelope Play," *American Forests* 86 (July 1980): 30–33+.

Diamond, Jared. "The American Blitzkrieg: A Mammoth Undertaking," *Discover* 8 (June 1987): 82–88.

Dooling, Anna. "Plight of the Prairie Chicken." *Boulder Daily Camera.* (May 10, 1984): B-1.

Feucht, James R. "How Drought Affects Plants." *Colorado Green* (Winter 1987): 60–67.

Hinchman, Steve. "Endangered Ferrets Will Be Rounded Up." *High Country News* 18 (Sept. 29, 1986): 13.

Jackson, Wes and Marty Bender. "New Roots for American Agriculture." *Journal of Soil and Water Conservation* 36 (November/December 1981): 320–324.

Johnson, Steve. "Allan Savory: Guru of False Hopes and an Overstocked Range." *High Country News* 19 (April 27, 1987): 10+.

Judd, B. I. "Plant Succession of Old Fields in the Dust Bowl." *Southwest Naturalist* 19 (September 1974): 227–239.

Krueger, K. "Feeding Relationships among Bison, Pronghorn, and Prairie Dogs: an Experimental Analysis." *Ecology* 67 (June 1986): 760–770.

Laycock, George. "Roger's Last Bird." *Audubon* 84 (May 1982): 26–31.

Lee, Ernest, Ed. "A Woman on the Buffalo Range: the Journal of Ella Dumont." *West Texas Historical Association Year Book* (1964): 146–167.

Leydet, Francois and Terrence Moore. "A Place of Subtle Beauty." *Audubon* 84 (November 1982): 72–80.

Livingston, R. B. "Relict True Prairie Communities in Central Colorado." *Ecology* 33 (October 1952): 72–86.

Luoma, Jon R. "Discouraging Words." *Audubon* 88 (September 1986): 86–104.

McDonnell, Doris. "Agony of Dust-bowl Years Recalled." *The Denver Post* (May 1, 1982): B-3.

Oakley, Glenn. "Allan Savory's Range Revolution." *Sierra* 71 (November/December 1986): 26–30.

Paul, Alex H. "Across the 49th: Thunderstorms in the Northern Great Plains." *Great Plains Quarterly* 3 (Fall 1983): 195–204.

Reichhardt, K. L. "Succession of Abandoned Fields on the Shortgrass Prairie, Northeastern Colorado." *Southwest Naturalist* 27 (1982): 299–304.

Risser, James. "The Other Farm Crisis." *Sierra* 70 (May/June 1985): 40–47.

Sinclair, Ward. "Keeping Soil Down on the Farm." *Sierra* 72 (May/June 1987): 26–29.

Skovlin, Jon. "Southern Africa's Experience with Intensive Short Duration Grazing." *Rangelands* 9 (August 1987): 162–166.

PAMPHLETS AND UNPUBLISHED MATERIAL

Armstrong, David M. and Jerry Freeman. "Preliminary Report: Mammals of the Boulder Creek Cottonwood Grove." Report to City of Boulder, Colorado, 1984.

Fitzgerald, James P., ed. *Grassland Institute Information Book.* Denver: Denver Audubon Society, 1986.

Thacker, Robert. "The Plains Landscape and Descriptive Technique." *Great Plains Quarterly* 2 (Summer 1982): 146–155.

Uresk, D. W., J. G. MacCracken, and A. J. Bjugstad. "Prairie Dog Density and Cattle Grazing Relationships." *Proc. Great Plains Wildlife Damage Control Workshop.* Univ. of Nebraska, Lincoln 5 (1982): 199–201.

Wallach, Bret. "The Return of the Prairie." *Landscape* 28 (1985): 1–5.

Wells, Philip V. "Postglacial Vegetational History of the Great Plains." *Science* 167 (March 1970): 1574–1582.

Wells, Philip V. "Scarp Woodlands, Transported Grassland Soils, and Concept of Grassland Climate in the Great Plains Region." *Science* 148 (April 1965): 246–249.

Wicklow, D. T., Rabinder Kumar, and J. E. Lloyd. "Germination of Blue Grama Seeds Buried by Dung Beetles." *Environmental Entomology* 13 (October 1984): 878–881.

Williams, Ted. "The Final Ferret Fiasco." *Audubon* 88 (May 1986): 110–119.

Williams, Ted and Lawrence B. McQueen. "Solid Gold Sphinx." *Audubon* 88 (March 1986): 100–103.

Wisehart, M. K. "Wichita Bill, Cowboy Artist, Rode into the Halls of Fame." *American Magazine* (August 1927): 34+.

Yates, Steve. "Windspirit of the West." *Audubon* 87 (May 1985): 42–47.

Zimmerman, Gregory M., Harold Goetz and Paul W. Mielke, Jr. "Use of an Improved Statistical Method for Group Comparisons to Study Effects of Prairie Fire." *Ecology* 66 (April 1985): 606–611.

Indeck, Jeff. "Sediment Analysis and Mammalian Fauna From Little Box Elder Cave, Wyoming." Ph.D. diss., Univ. of Colorado at Boulder, 1987.

Jones, Stephen R. "Hawks, Eagles, and Prairie Dogs: Wintering Raptors in Boulder County, Colorado." Publication No. 9. Boulder: Boulder County Nature Assoc., 1987.

Maxwell, Martha. Papers. Colorado Historical Society, Denver.

Walker, Danny N. "Studies on the Late Pleistocene Mammalian Fauna of Wyoming." Ph.D. diss., Univ. of Wyoming, 1986.

GOVERNMENT DOCUMENTS

Chronic, John and Halka Chronic, "Prairie, Peak, and Plateau; a Guide to the Geology of Colorado." *Colorado. Geological Survey. Bulletin 32* (1972).

Colorado. Dept. of Agriculture. Resource Analysis Section. *Colorado High Plains Study: Summary Report.* Denver: 1983.

U.S. Congress. House. Committee on Government Operations. *Federal Grazing Program: All Is Not Well On The Range.* Washington, D.C.: GPO, 1986.

U.S. Dept. of Agriculture. *Yearbook.* Washington, D.C.: GPO, 1896.

U.S. Dept. of Agriculture. Forest Service. *The National Grasslands of the Rocky Mountain Region.* Washington, D.C.: GPO, 1985.

U.S. Dept. of the Interior. National Park Service. *Identification of Prairie in National Park Units* by James Stubbendieck. (National Park Service Occasional Papers #7). Washington, D.C.: GPO, 1986.

U.S. Dept. of the Interior. National Park Service. *Prospector, Cowhand and Sodbuster* by Robert Ferris. Washington, D.C.: GPO, 1967.

Stephen R. Jones is a Boulder, Colorado, school-teacher and naturalist who has studied and photographed prairie wildlife for fifteen years. He has received national recognition for his efforts to preserve wildlife habitats on the High Plains.

Ruth Carol Cushman is a freelance nature writer and a part-time reference librarian at the University of Colorado. She and her husband, Glenn, enjoy backpacking, ski touring, traveling, and simply watching the wildlife in their Boulder backyard.